Stock Dividends in Germany
An Empirical Analysis

Studienreihe der Stiftung Kreditwirtschaft an der Universität Hohenheim

Herausgeber:

Prof. Dr. Hans-Peter Burghof

Band 50

Dirk Sturz

Stock Dividends in Germany

An Empirical Analysis

Verlag Wissenschaft & Praxis

Bibliografische Information der Deutschen Nationalbibliothek

Die Deutsche Nationalbibliothek verzeichnet diese Publikation in der Deutschen Nationalbibliografie; detaillierte bibliografische Daten sind im Internet über http://dnb.dnb.de abrufbar.

D100
ISBN 978-3-89673-687-1

D-75447 Sternenfels, Nußbaumweg 6
Tel. +49 7045 930093 Fax +49 7045 930094
verlagwp@t-online.de www.verlagwp.de

Druck und Bindung: Esser printSolutions GmbH, Bretten

Ef' liba n'e lon, watra sa tingi.

Preface

Stock distributions change the number of outstanding shares and the equity structure of a firm. From a neoclassic perspective, both effects should not affect the market value. However, empirical studies find overwhelming evidence, that the stock price of companies reacts significantly positive to the announcement of stock distributions.

Despite the broad consensus about the positive market reaction, the possible causes are still at issue. Focusing on stock dividends, which are a special type of stock distributions, this study revisits this puzzle and investigates especially the economic effects of changes in the equity structure.

The investigation of the theoretical explanations discussed in the literature against the background of US- and German law concludes that these explanations are only resilient in the legal framework of Germany. This result is surprising since these theories were developed specially for the US market.

This is one of different reasons why German data is highly suitable for this study. Beyond that, German stock dividends allow to solely change the equity structure without issuing new shares. In prior empirical studies, both effects are diluted.

The empirical investigation provides a deeper insight into the economics of stock dividends. Beyond analyzing existing theories, additional explanations of the effects are developed and tested. I hope that this volume of the study series of the Stiftung Kreditwirtschaft finds your interest.

October 2014, Stuttgart

Prof. Dr. Hans-Peter Burghof

Table of Contents

Tables

Figures

I Introduction

This study investigates the announcement effects of stock dividends, a special type of stock distributions in Germany. Stock distributions in general can be described as the issuance of bonus shares to shareholders. As these bonus shares are distributed to the old shareholders free of charge, no additional capital is paid into the company. Neglecting transaction costs, stock distributions do not affect cash flow, assets or the debt equity ratio of the firm. Hence, the market value of firms announcing stock distributions should remain constant.

Regarding the accounting method, stock distributions can be separated into stock splits and stock dividends. While stock splits simply increase the number of shares without affecting the balance sheet, stock dividends increase capital stock from corporate funds, such as capital reserves or retained earnings. Modigliani/Miller (1958) have shown that when the debt equity ratio is irrelevant for the firm value, any transaction within the equity item of the balance sheet should be irrelevant as well.

Consequently, there should be no impact on stock prices following announcements of stock distributions. On the ex-day of the stock distribution, the share price should decrease at the same rate at which the number of shares increases to keep the market value constant. Yet a notable number of empirical studies find significant positive abnormal returns following the announcement of stock distributions. The studies cited are Fama et al. (1969), Woolridge (1983b), Grinblatt/Masulis/Titman (1984) and Brennan/Copeland (1988b). Few studies which investigate the German market confirm these results (Gebhardt/Entrup/Heiden, 1994, Padberg, 1995, Kaserer/Brunner, 1997).

Theories that literature provides to explain the positive announcement effects can be categorized into liquidity-based explanations and signaling theory.

The liquidity-based trading range hypothesis by Copeland (1979) claims that an optimal price band for stocks exists. High share prices decrease the divisibility and thereby small investments in the stock are hindered. When stock prices exceed the upper boundary of the band, managers can reduce the share price by stock distributions to increase the liquidity of the stock.

In contrast to the trading range hypothesis, the retained earnings hypothesis by Grinblatt/Masulis/Titman (1984) is based on the signaling theory and thereby focuses on the accounting method and not on the issuance of bonus shares. Thus, the retained earnings hypothesis can only be applied to stock dividends, not to stock splits.

A brief description of the retained earnings hypothesis can be found in Rankine/Stice (1997b: 165). They summarize the retained earnings hypothesis as follows: "By voluntarily reducing the existing pool of distributable funds, managers of undervalued firms can signal their confidence that such a reduction will not negatively impact the firm's ability to make future cash distributions."

Nevertheless, the effects of the accounting method are not yet completely understood. To provide deeper insight, this study focuses on the analysis of stock dividends. First of all, it is questionable whether distributable funds indeed are reduced by stock dividends. Therefore, *Chapter II* illustrates the detailed mechanisms of stock distributions and how distributable funds are restricted by stock dividends in the US and in Germany.

Chapter III discusses theories and empirical findings of stock dividends. As none of the studies finds negative abnormal returns, theory focuses on the positive effects of the accounting method. Therefore, literature has not yet considered that the management of a firm with high free cash flow can further deprive capital from the shareholders by transferring retained earnings to capital stock. Following Jensen (1986), this negative effect should be particularly significant for firms with a high free cash flow.

Chapters II and *III* conclude that analyzing the German market is more promising than the US market for a variety of reasons. First of all, it is questionable whether distributable funds truly are restricted by stock dividends in the US. Second, the accounting method of stock distributions often is not clearly defined in many US announcements. Therefore, the announcement effects of the accounting method are diluted in the US.

Chapter IV and *V* utilize an event study to investigate stock dividends in Germany empirically. This study focuses solely on the accounting method disregarding liquidity effects. Different hypotheses which are developed in the previous chapters, such as Jensen's free cash flow hypothesis, are incorporated into the empirical analysis. Beyond it has not yet been possible to empirically analyze the accounting effect separately from the liquidity effect as stock dividends in prior studies always issued bonus shares at the same time. Up to now, this is the main criticism on the retained earnings hypothesis. Since 1998, Germany allows for stock dividends without the issuance of bonus shares (Wulff, 2001: 19), which will be investigated separately.

Chapter VI summarizes and discusses the main results of the study.

II Regulatory Framework

II.1 Basic Conditions

II.1.a Stock Dividends, Stock Splits and Accounting

In the United States, the American Institute of Certified Public Accountants (AICPA) separates stock distributions into two different categories (Accounting Research Bulletin (ARB) 43 Chapter 7B). The first type is the stock dividend and the second type is the stock split-up (stock splits). AICPA bases the differentiation on the motivation of management to issue bonus shares. Even though AICPA recognizes that the issuance of bonus shares does not transfer any assets from the corporation to the shareholders, AICPA believes that shareholders do regard bonus shares as a distribution of firm assets (section 10). Consequently, AICPA defines issues of bonus shares which aim for giving shareholders the impression of getting a distribution of assets as stock dividends. Because of the classification of stock dividends as a distribution, the amount of the fair value of the issuance (not only the par value) should be transferred from retained earnings (earned surplus) to capital stock.

The second motivation to issue bonus shares which AICPA takes into consideration is the decrease of the share price to improve marketability. Issuances which are based on this motivation are called stock splits (stock split-ups). In this case, no balance sheet transaction is necessary (*section 11*). As it is obviously difficult to observe the motivation of managers, AICPA says that issuances with ratios of less than 20% to 25% are likely to be stock dividends and issuances with higher ratios are likely to be stock splits. AICPA argues that low split ratios are less capable to reduce the share price than high split ratios (*section 16*).

AICPA also lists a third form of stock distributions. Large stock dividends (split-up effected in the form of a dividend) with a split ratio higher than 25 percent reduce the market price while capital stock is increased. In contrast to the stock dividend, capital stock is only increased by the par value of the bonus shares. Additionally, capital stock can be funded from capital reserve, not only from retained earnings (*section 11*).

Obviously, the choice of the accounting method is not completely left to management. In practice, the accounting of stock distributions mainly depends on the split ratio. Hence, a firm which splits its stock at a low rate is forced to increase capital stock even if managers would prefer to split without any changes on the balance sheet.

In contrast to the US method, the German stock corporation act (Aktiengesetz, AktG) leaves the choice of the accounting method to management independent of the split ratio. When the capital stock is increased from corporate funds, the transaction is called a *Kapitalerhöhung aus Gesellschaftsmitteln* (German stock dividend). Due to the accounting method, the stock dividend is quite similar to the US stock dividend. The major difference is that in Germany, par values are always relevant, while for small stock dividends in the US, capital stock has to be increased by the fair value. When bonus shares are issued to stockholders without any transfer on the balance sheet, the transaction is called *Aktiensplit*, which is the German stock split.

Wulff (2001: 19 et seqq.) and Harrison (2000: 47 et seqq.) describe the historical legal development of the stock dividend. Before the end of 1959, capital stock could not be increased directly from retained earnings. Until then, retained earnings had to be distributed to the shareholders in a first step and then in a second step deposited in capital stock by an equity issuance. As tax had to be paid on the dividends, the transaction was rather expensive at that time. The stock dividend was introduced to the regulatory framework in 1959 and has beenpart of the AktG since 1965. There, the stock dividend is regulated in sections 207 to 220 of the AktG.

The AktG allows stock dividends only when the following preconditions are met:

1. Has to be approved by at least 75% of the shareholders meeting (§§ 207 I, 182 I AktG)
2. No accumulated deficit and net loss for the year (§ 208 II 1 AktG)

To understand the manifold accounting effects of stock dividends in Germany, first the equity structure must be illustrated. The structure of equity on the balance sheet of German stock corporations can be found in the German commercial code (§ 266 II 3 HGB).

I. Capital stock

II. Capital reserve

III. Retained earnings

III.1 Legal reserve

III.2 Reserves for own shares

III.3 Statutory reserve

III.4 Other retained earnings

IV. Accumulated profit/deficit

V. Net income/loss for the year

Stock dividends always increase *capital stock (I)*, but the sources can vary. The disposition of the different sources is regulated in § 208 I 2 AktG. Potential sources are capital reserve (II), legal reserve (III.1) or other retained earnings (III.4). Other retained earnings (III.4) can be transferred without further obligations. Capital reserve (II) and/or legal reserves (III.1) can only be transferred into capital stock as long as capital reserve and legal reserve together remain at least at a 10 percent level of capital stock.

Condition 1:

$$capital\ reserve\ (II) + legal\ reserve\ (III.1) \geq$$

$$0.1\ \times capital\ stock\ (I)$$[1]

Table 1 summarizes the classification of stock splits and stock dividends in dependence of the accounting treatment and the split ratio for the US and for Germany.

[1] A higher boundary can be defined in the articles of association (§§ 150 II, 208 I 2 AktG)

Accounting treatment		Germany	US	
		Classification independent of split ratio	*Change in the number of shares in x %*	
			0 % < x < 20-25 %	*x > 20 - 25 %*
No accounting		Stock split	-	Stock split
Reduction by fair value of	*Capital Reserve*	-	(Small) stock dividend	-
	Legal Reserve	-	-	-
	Other Retained Earnings	-	-	-
Reduction by par value of	*Capital Reserve*	Stock dividend	-	Large stock dividend
	Legal Reserve	Stock dividend	-	-
	Other Retained Earnings	Stock dividend	-	Large stock dividend

Table 1: Classification of Stock Splits and Stock Dividends in Germany and the US (own illustration according to Gebhardt/Entrup/Heiden (1994: 312) and Wulff (2002: 25)).

II.1.b Bonus Shares

Regardless of choice, whether capital stock is increased from other retained earnings, legal reserves, capital reserves or a combination of these, management in Germany can choose whether to issue bonus shares or not.

The issuance of bonus shares was a mandatory component for stock dividends in Germany until April 1998 (Wulff, 2001: 19). The reason for this can be found in the Stock Corporation Act which only allowed par value shares before 1998. As each par value share represents a fixed amount (par value) of the total capital stock, the increase in capital stock has to be adjusted by the issuance of new shares. In contrast, no-par shares represent a certain fraction and not a fixed amount of the capital stock. Therefore, the number of (no-par) shares is not necessarily adjusted when capital stock is increased from corporate funds. The introduction of no-par shares in 1998 allows corporations that converted their par value shares to no-par shares to forgo the issuance of bonus shares when they increase their capital stock from corporate funds. Then, the par value is increased by a stock dividend.

In any case, as the issuance of bonus shares only increases the number of outstanding shares, the firm value should not be affected. As the share price is calculated by dividing the market value of equity by the (increased) number of shares, the share price should decrease at the same rate as the number of shares increases at the ex-date of the issuance.

II.1.c Effects on the Par Value

Due to the different accounting methods, stock splits and stock dividends have different effects on the par value *PV* of a firm, which, in Germany, is the capital stock per share.

Subsequently it will be shown how stock splits and stock dividends in dependency of the issuance of bonus shares affect the par value.

Formula 1:

$$PV = \frac{CS}{NS}$$

Where CS is capital stock

NS is the number of common shares

1. Stock dividends without bonus shares

   When capital stock is increased by x-percent without the issuance of bonus shares, the par value change is given by

   Formula 2:

$$\Delta(PV)^{no\ bonus\ shares} = \frac{PV^{new}}{PV^{old}} - 1 = \frac{(1+x) \times CS/_{NS}}{CS/_{NS}} - 1 = x$$

   Hence, the par value increases at the same rate at which capital stock is issued.

2. Stock Dividends with bonus shares

   When bonus shares are issues, capital stock is increased at the same rate as the number of shares and thus the par value remains constant.

Formula 3:

$$\Delta(PV)^{bonus\,shares} = \frac{PV^{new}}{PV^{old}} - 1$$

$$= \frac{(1+x) \times CS / (1+x) \times NS}{CS / NS} - 1 = 0$$

3. Stock splits

   Stock splits always lead to a reduction of the par value as the following equation shows.

Formula 4:

$$\Delta(PV)^{stock\,split} = \frac{PV^{new}}{PV^{old}} - 1 = \frac{CS / (1+x) \times NS}{CS / NS} - 1 = -\frac{x}{1+x}$$

The varying effects of stock splits, stock dividends with bonus shares and stock dividends without bonus shares cause further constraints.

As stock splits always reduce the par value and the par value is limited to a minimum of 1 Euro[2] (§ 8 II 1 AktG), stock splits are not allowed when the par value of the firm would be reduced beneath 1 Euro. The only way for those firms to increase the number of common shares is the stock dividend.

---

[2] For no-par shares, the implicit par value which is calculated by dividing the common stock by the number of common shares must be higher than 1 Euro as well (§ 9 III 3 AktG).

Data shows that this restriction is relevant for most firms in Germany. Before the minimum par value was lowered from 50 DM to 5 DM in 1994, the par value of 94 percent of the firms listed on the Frankfurt Stock Exchange in 1993 was already at the minimum par value (Wulff, 2002: 273).

Consequently, the number of stock splits in Germany was especially high in years when the minimum par value was reduced[3] (Gebhardt/Entrup/Heiden, 1994: 312 and Wulff, 2001: 26). The distribution of stock splits and stock dividends in Germany in time is listed in *Appendix 1*. For the US, the distribution of stock splits in time can be found in Fama et al. (1969: 12). In contrast, Wulff (2002: 272) states the following in regards to the US: "Usually the par value is very low and – most importantly – does not prevent the company from deciding on a stock split or choosing a convenient split factor"[4].

Additionally, only certain split ratios were allowed for stock splits between 1953 and 1996. Between 1966 and 1994, stock splits could only be used to double the number of common shares as only certain par values were allowed (Wulff (2001: 26). As the par value is not affected for stock dividends when bonus shares are issued[5], the percentage of new shares was more flexible for stock dividends than for stock splits in that period.

II.2 Further Legal Implications

II.2.a Restrictions for Future Equity Issuances

Besides the restrictions on the payout policy which arise from stock dividends, management is constrained by the rules for the issuance of new shares. § 9 I AktG determines that the issuance of new shares is prohibited when the issuance price is lower than the par value. Likewise, this is

[3] An overview over the historical development of minimum par values is described by Wulff (2001: 28 et seqq. and 2002: 272 et seqq.) and Harrison (2000: 32 et seqq.). Starting at 100 DM in 1949, the par value was decreased in several steps to 1 Euro in 1999.

[4] The US regulation determines no minimum par value (Wulff, 2001: 26).

[5] The issuance of bonus shares was mandatory at that time.

applied to no-par shares by calculating the implicit par value (capital stock divided by the number of shares).

The risk that this rule is applied rises when the share price gets closer to the par value and thus the proportion declines.

Formula 5:

$$\frac{P}{PV} = \frac{MV/_{NS}}{CS/_{NS}}$$

Where P is the share price

PV is the par value

NS is the number of common shares

$MV = P \times NS$ is the market value of common equity

$CS = PV \times NS$ is the capital stock

Formula 5, analogous to *Chapter II.1.c*, can be used to analyze how stock dividends and stock splits affect this fraction. For stock dividends, it has to be taken into consideration whether the stock dividend includes the issuance of bonus shares or not.

1. Stock dividends without bonus shares

   Assuming capital stock is increased by x-percent, the only variable which changes is the common stock CS. The relative change of the ratio $\frac{P}{PV}$ can be calculated as follows:

Formula 6:

$$\Delta\left(\frac{P}{PV}\right)^{no\ bonus\ shares} = \frac{\left(\frac{P}{PV}\right)^{new}}{\left(\frac{P}{PV}\right)^{old}} - 1 = \frac{\frac{MV/NS}{(1+x)\times CS/NS}}{\frac{MV/NS}{CS/NS}} - 1$$

$$= -\frac{x}{1+x} < 0$$

$$for\ x > 0$$

Where x is the percentage increase of capital stock

2. Stock dividends with bonus shares

   When capital stock is increased by x-percent and at the same time, bonus shares are issued at the same extent, the ratio $\frac{P}{PV}$ changes at exactly the same rate as for stock dividends without bonus shares:

Formula 7:

$$\Delta\left(\frac{P}{PV}\right)^{bonus\ shares} = \frac{\left(\frac{P}{PV}\right)^{new}}{\left(\frac{P}{PV}\right)^{old}} - 1 = \frac{\frac{MV/(1+x)\times NS}{(1+x)\times CS/(1+x)\times NS}}{\frac{MV/NS}{CS/NS}} - 1$$

$$= -\frac{x}{1+x} < 0$$

$$for\ x > 0$$

3. Stock splits

When stocks are simply split without any changes on the balance sheet, the change of the ratio $\frac{P}{PV}$ is given by

Formula 8:

$$\Delta(\frac{P}{PV})^{stock\ split} = \frac{(\frac{P}{PV})^{new}}{(\frac{P}{PV})^{old}} - 1 = \frac{\frac{MV/(1+x)\times NS}{CS/(1+x)\times NS}}{\frac{MV/NS}{CS/NS}} - 1 = 0$$

Formulas 6, 7 and 8 show, that the risk that equity issues are prohibited because the issuance price is lower than the par value increases only for stock dividends, not for stock splits. The ratio $\frac{P}{PV}$ declines independently from the issuance of bonus shares at the rate $-\frac{x}{1+x}$. *Formula 8* reveals that stock splits have no influence on the options of the firm to issue equity.

It is questionable, however, whether the increase of the risk that an equity issue might fail is of economical significance. The importance of the prohibition to issues under par value rises for small $\frac{P}{PV}$. While healthy firms are assumed to have a high ratio $\frac{P}{PV}$ and thus are not affected by this regulation, it is more important for distressed firms. But as mentioned in *Chapter II.1.a*, stock distributions are anyway prohibited for most distressed firms (§ 208 II 1 AktG).

II.2.b Distribution of Funds

To understand how stock dividends restrict the payout policy, a closer look at the legal aspects of profit distribution in Germany is needed. § 58 IV AktG defines that shareholders have a claim on the balance sheet profit[6]. The shareholders annual meeting decides about the distribution of the balance sheet profit (§ 174 I AktG). The calculation of the balance sheet profit is regulated in § 158 I AktG.

	Net income/loss for the year (V)
+/-	*Prior years' accumulated profit/deficit (IV)*
+	Reduction of *capital reserve (II)*
+	Reduction of *retained earnings (III)*
-	Increase of *retained earnings (III)*
=	Balance sheet profit

Table 2: Calculation of the Balance Sheet Profit (Heiden, 2002: 7).

As shareholders only have claims on the balance sheet profit and not on the *net income for the year (V)*, the scope of action of managers on the calculation of the balance sheet profit must be illustrated. When calculating the balance sheet profit, legal requirements to the profit distribution must be satisfied in a first step. Then the board of directors and the supervisory board can dispose of the profit to a certain level.

[6] Restrictions to the general claims of shareholders on the balance sheet profit arise from § 58 III, IV AktG.

The following illustrates these steps:

1. 5 percent of the *net income for the year (V)* minus the prior years' accumulated *deficit (IV)* has to be converted into the *legal reserve (III.1)*. This is mandatory as long as *Condition 1* is not satisfied (§ 150 II AktG).

   Formula 9:

$$\Delta\, legal\, reserve\, (III.1)_t \; = \; 0.05 \times (net\, income\, of\, the\, year\, (V)_t - accumulated\, deficit\, (IV)_{t-1})$$

2. The board of directors and the supervisory board can transfer up to 50 percent of the annual surplus remaining after 1. into *other retained earnings (III.4)* (§ 58 II 1 AktG).

   Formula 10:

$$\Delta\, other\, retained\, earnings\, (III.4)_t^{management} \; \leq \; 0.5 \times (net\, income\, of\, the\, year\, (V)_t - accumulated\, deficit\, (IV)_{t-1} - \Delta\, legal\, reserve\, (III.1)_t)$$

   A smaller or larger percentage (more than 50 percent) can be defined in the articles of association (§ 58 II 2 AktG). But, as soon as retained earnings (III.4) exceed 50 percent of capital stock (I), the amount which the board of directors and the supervisory board can transfer is again limited to a maximum of 50 percent as *Formula 10* shows. Wulff (2001: 20) argues that managers might use stock dividend to regain more control over profit distribution. Obviously, managers have a substantial influence on the distributable amount[7].

3. The board of directors makes a proposal for the disposition of the the annual surplus remaining after 1. and 2. to the annual shareholders meeting (§§ 170 II, 173 AktG). This proposal contains further transformations into retained earnings and the amount of dividends. If the desired payout sum exceeds the remaining annual surplus and the accumulated profit, *other retained earnings (III.4)* can be distributed.

   Besides stock dividends, the *capital reserve (II)* and the *legal reserve (III.1)* can only be reduced to compensate a negative sum of *net income/loss for the year (V)* plus *prior years' accumulated profit/deficit (IV)*. Thus, while the *capital reserve (II)* and the *legal reserve (III.1)* are not directly distributable, they have indirect positive effects on the distributional funds as they can be used to prevent a reduction of distributable *other retained earnings (III.4)* caused by losses. *Other retained earnings (III.4)* can only then be distributed in the year of the same year when *Condition 1* holds after the reduction of capital reserves or legal reserves (§ 150 III, IV AktG). If *Condition 1* is not satisfied, the other retained earnings saved can be distributed in future periods (Heiden, 2002: 7).

As § 150 III, IV AktG stipulates, the *capital reserve (II)* and the *legal reserve (III.1)* cannot be distributed to shareholders directly. The only way to distribute these equity items is to first transform *capital reserves (II)* and/or *legal reserves (III.1)* into *capital stock (I)* by a stock dividend and then distribute the capital stock by a capital reduction (§§ 222 – 228 AktG). Equally, the stock dividend capital reductions can be determined only by a majority of at least 75 percent of the shareholders meeting (§§ 182 I, 207 I, 222 1 AktG) as long as the protection rules for creditors are respected (§§ 225, 237 AktG). Thus, the legal requirements to distribute *capital reserves (III)* or *legal reserves (III.1)* even (slightly) higher than for the distribution of *capital stock (I)*.

---

[7] Additionally, managers can influence the *net income/loss for the year (V)* by the specific application of accounting options (Heiden, 2002: 5).

Additionally, stockholders in Germany can enforce the payout of at least 4 percent of the capital stock as long as there is no conflict between the payout and legal or economical constraints (§ 254 I AktG).

The payout restrictions caused by stock dividends in the US are not that clear. Crawford, Franz and Lobo (2005: 535) analyze whether stock dividends cause dividend constraints on account of the statutes of incorporation. They find that regulation differs tremendously between the US states. While in California payouts primarily are limited to retained earnings, Delaware is more liberal. Delaware is of special importance according to Jiraporn and Gleason: "Delaware incorporation is dominant in the U.S.; more than 50% of publicly traded firms are incorporated in Delaware." (2007: 40). In Delaware, any surplus can be distributed to stock holders independently from the amount of retained earnings[8]. As the amount of distributable funds is thus completely independent from retained earnings. Crawford, Franz and Lobo (2005) conclude that Delaware's statutes of incorporation do not narrow the ability to distribute cash to stock holders after a stock dividend.

Following the basic consideration of Crawford, Franz and Lobo (2005), the reduction of retained earnings does not lead to additional constraints on the payout policy in Delaware. However the increase of capital stock does. The distributable surplus is defined as the difference between the market value of net assets and capital stock (Crawford/Franz/Lobo: 2005: 535). Consequently, stock dividends do not reduce distributable funds by reducing retained earnings, but might be diminished by increasing capital stock.

Roberts et al. (1990: 43) observed that capital stock is in fact not directly distributable. Regardless, managers have broad latitude to reallocate between capital stock, capital reserve and retained earnings.

Referring to McGough (1988) and Roberts et al. (1990), Leuz, Deller and Stubenrath (1998: 114) conclude that capital stock cannot constrict distribution of funds effectively.

---

[8] A more detailed description of legal dividend constraints in different US states is given by Leuz, Deller and Stubenrath (1998: 113 et seq.), McDaniel (1996), McGough (1988) and Roberts et al. (1990).

II.3 Conclusions

This conclusion summarizes and discusses the main differences in stock splits and stock dividends in the US and Germany. For Germany, an overview is given in *Table 4*.

Accounting methods and legal restrictions of stock distributions are rather heterogeneous among the US states. This aggravates a profound analysis of the regulatory framework in the US.

Nevertheless, it can be concluded that in the US and in Germany stock splits and stock dividends are distinguished by the accounting method. While stock dividends change the equity structure as shown in *Chapter* II.2.a, stock splits do not influence the balance sheet at all.

In Germany, stock dividends constrain distributable funds. These constraints are especially strong when retained earnings are reduced. A reduction of capital reserves or legal reserves limits the firms' payout policy only indirectly. The extent of the reduction of retained earnings or capital reserves is primarily determined by the split ratio.

For the US, literature provides no definite insight on whether regulation imposes that distributable funds are limited through stock dividends. However, it holds unanimously that the degree of dividend constraints differs from state to state (Rankine/Stice 1997a 26). When dividend constraints exist, they affect small stock dividends in a specific way, as a higher amount (the fair value instead of the par value) must then be transferred into capital stock.

In the US, split ratios are not constrained. In contrast, German law limits split ratios by a minimum par value for stock splits and for stock dividends by the availability of funds which can be transferred into capital stock. Consequently, split ratios tend to be smaller in Germany than in the US, as a comparison of the findings of Gebhardt, Entrup and Heiden (1994: 312) for Germany and Grinblatt, Titmann and Masulis, (1984: 467) for the US indicates in *Table 3*.

New Shares / Old Shares	German Stock Dividends	US Stock Distributions
0 - 10 percent	26%	12%
10 - 25 percent	48%	10%
25 - 50 percent	19%	3%
50 - 100 percent	6%	69%
> 100 percent	1%	6%

Table 3: Comparison of Split Ratios in Germany and the US (Gebhardt/Entrup/Heiden, 1994: 312, Grinblatt/Titmann/Masulis, 1984: 467).

As par values in Germany are usually noted at the lowest legal level, stock splits are prohibited for most firms and therefore are mainly driven by legistlative reductions of the minimum par value. Then the split ratios are exceptionally high when the minimum par value is lowered extensively. Therefore, German stock splits are excluded from *Table 3* to avoid a distortion of the illustration.

Furthermore, effects of the accounting treatment of stock dividends can arise from debt covenants when they include constraints which are linked to affected items on the balance sheet. The relevance of debt covenants for the US and Germany will be discussed in *Chapter III.1.b.2.1.*

	Stock Dividends		Stock Splits
Preconditions	Majority of at least 75 % of the annual shareholders meeting		Majority of at least 75 % of the annual shareholders meeting
	Enough funds (other retained earnings, capital reserves and/or legal reserves)		Par value must be higher than the minimum par value
	No accumulated net deficit and net loss for the year		Only certain Split Ratios allowed before 1997

Consequences	***Reduction of Other Retained Earnings***	***Reduction of Capital Reserves and/or Legal Reserves***	
	Direct reduction of distributable funds	Indirect reduction of distributable funds	
	Issuance of Bonus Shares	***No Issuance of Bonus Shares***	
	No influence on the par value	Increase of the par value	Decrease of the par value
	Share price declines proportionally to the split ratio		Share price declines proportionally to the split ratio
	No influence on future equity issuances	Future equity issuances alleviated	Future equity issuances aggravated

Table 4: Preconditions and Consequences of Stock Dividends and Stock Splits in Germany.

III Theory and Empirical Evidence

III.1 Theoretical Considerations on Stock Distributions

III.1.a Classification of Existing Approaches

Many studies analyze the stock market impact of stock distributions empirically. All major studies observe positive abnormal returns in the announcement period. These findings are robust for different countries. A discussion of empirical evidence will take place in *Chapter III.2*.

While the positive market reaction is undisputed, literature does not agree about the reasons. *Chapter III.1* will discuss the current approaches which exist for the US and analyze whether they are applicable for Germany as well.

As equity structure which is effected by stock dividends is a subcategory of the capital structure of a firm, the starting point of theoretical analysis of stock distributions is the famous study of 1958, Modigliani and Miller. In their analysis, Modigliani and Miller investigate the impact of the capital structure of a firm on its market value. Modigliani and Miller create a model in which capital structure is irrelevant. This model is comprised of the following assumptions:

1. Information Symmetry
2. Perfect capital markets
3. No taxes
4. No bankruptcy costs

However, multiple empirical studies show that capital structure does indeed matter. To find explanations, one can eliminate single assumptions in the Miller/Modigliani model to identify effects on the firm's value.

The two major explanations for the influence of stock distribution on the firms' value are the retained earnings hypothesis and the trading range hypothesis which focus on the first two assumptions of Modigliani and Miller.

Assuming information asymmetry between managers and investors, Fama et al. (1969) analyze whether stock splits reveal additional information to investors. Copeland (1979) argues that due to imperfect capital markets, frictions such as transaction costs and limited divisibility of shares cause the effects of stock distributions on the share price. The following chapters will illustrate the theories. As they are developed for the US market, the theories will, firstly, be described against the US background. Secondly, it will be discussed whether and to what extent the theories can be applied to the German market.

III.1.b Signaling Theory

III.1.b.1 Fundamentals of Signaling

Fama et al. (1969) find that stock splits often are followed by dividend increases and thus reason that stock splits are a signal for higher dividends. Hence, the positive market reaction to the announcement of stock splits is not caused by the transaction itself, but rather by the revealed information. This hypothesis is supported by their empirical results which show that the positive cumulative abnormal returns (*CAR*s) disappear when the expectations of the investors concerning the dividends are not satisfied. But as the fundamentals of signaling theory were settled in 1973 by Spence and applied to financial markets by Ross (1977), Leland/Pyle (1977) and Bhattacharya (1979), the study of Fama et al. does not yet deliver a profound explanation or analysis as to whether stock distributions are credible signals for high future earnings.

The signaling theory assumes that managers have more or better information than investors. As managers are controlled by investors and oftentimes have financial incentives which are linked to the company's performance, managers have a high incentive to transfer positive information to the investors. Due to moral hazard, investors might overstate their assessment of the firm's prospect (Leland/Pyle, 1977: 371). Therefore, managers can send signals about their private information. To be credible, these signals have to restrain moral hazard and hence have to be costly. These costs have to be low enough for good firms to bear them and have to be high enough for bad firms to prevent them from also sending the signal.

Gebhardt, Entrup and Heiden (1994: 314) question why managers do not simply state their expectations. They refer to Penman (1983) who shows that earnings forecasts by management contain more information than dividend announcements. But as Grinblatt, Masulis and Titman note (1984: 464), management still might prefer sending signals rather than communicating directly as managers can be held liable for direct statements more than for signals.

III.1.b.2 Stock Distributions as Signals

III.1.b.2.1 Retained Earnings Hypothesis

The first study that applies the signaling theory to stock distributions and discusses the costs of false signaling is the study by Grinblatt, Masulis and Titman (1984). They state that due to the accounting method, stock dividends are credible signals. The basic idea is that firms will only reduce distributable funds voluntarily when they expect that future earnings will be high enough so that payouts can still be made. Assuming that stock dividends reduce distributable funds, only managers of firms with good prospects will issue stock dividends. Therefore, managers who want to convey their private information about good earnings prospects can intentionally use stock dividends to reveal their private information to less informed investors.

The pattern of stock dividends reducing retained earnings in the US is known as the retained earnings hypothesis. As the retained earnings hypothesis is based on the balance sheet transaction, this hypothesis can only be applied to stock dividends, not to stock splits. Subsequently, all signaling effects which are based on the accounting method will be subsumed under the retained earnings hypothesis.

However, since differences in payout restrictions among the US states are considerable as *Chapter II.2.b* shows, Crawford, Franz and Lobo (2005) question whether firms in more restrictive states such as California can avoid these payout restrictions. As California's firms can simply reincorporate in more liberal states such as Delaware, an upper boundary for costs of false signaling emerges. Since the direct costs of reincorporation are priced low at a median of 50,000 USD (2005: 536), this consideration could be feasible. But in addition to these low direct costs, further indirect costs such as a high tax level in Delaware and the "opportunity cost to a corporation of being domiciled in a state that is not its principle place of business" have to be incorporated (2005: 537). As these indirect costs are difficult to measure and are idiosyncratic for each company, it is hard to find evidence to support whether the total costs of reincorporation are high enough to avoid false signaling.

For Germany, stock dividends always reduce distributable funds. Regardless, the extent of the effect should be marginal when distributable funds remain high after the dividend. Gebhardt, Entrup and Heiden (1994: 315) suggest that the idiosyncratic constraint of dividends can be measured by the ratio of retained earnings per share divided by the last paid dividend per share.

However, Rankine and Stice (1997b: 165) state that in addition to legal dividend constraints, other costs of false signaling, such as other legal restrictions or debt covenants, have to be taken into consideration as well.

The characteristics of payout restrictions in US debt covenants have been studied in previous research. Smith and Warner (1979) analyze boilerplate debt covenants of the American Bar Foundation (1971). They observe that dividend payments there are restricted by (1979: 131 et seq.)

Formula 11:

$$D_T \leq max[0; k \sum_{t=0}^{T} E_t + \sum_{t=0}^{T} S_t - \sum_{t=0}^{T-1} D_t + F]$$

Where D_t are all distributions to shareholders in t

E_t is the net earnings in t

S_t is the net proceeds of stock sales

k and F are contract-specific constants

with $0 \leq k \leq 1$

Different studies find empirical evidence that a significant number of debt contracts do include payout restrictions as *Formula 11* shows. An overview is given in *Table 5*.

After analyzing if payout restrictions generally occur in debt covenants, the second question is whether these payout restrictions are affected by changes in retained earnings. As Smith and Warner (1979) and Kalay (1982) indicate, most payout restrictions are determined analogous to *Formula 11*. As Crawford, Franz and Lobo (2005: 533) remark, the distributions to shareholders do not include stock distributions. They conclude that "Also, as previous researchers find, none of the dividend constraints are based on retained earnings and none would have been affected by the accounting treatment selected for a stock distribution." (2005: 534). While the costs of false signaling in the retained earnings hypothesis obviously cannot be derived by direct dividend constraints in debt covenants, there still might be indirect dividend constraints. "Indirect dividend constraints are restrictions generated by items such as the contractual obligations of stockholders to maintain a minimum level of working capital or net worth and a minimum ratio of assets to liabilities." (Kalay, 1982: 218). However, as stock dividends only affect the ratio of the equity items, these indirect restrictions are not affected by stock distributions.

While Crawford, Franz and Lobo conclude that "Therefore, the stock distribution's accounting treatment cannot impose any costs on the firm related to its debt covenants." (2005: 535), debt covenants still can imply costs of false signaling other than payout restrictions. Duke and Hunt III (1990: 55) show in their sample that 55 percent of the firms do have restrictions for retained earnings. These restrictions are "...operationalized by requiring the firm to maintain a minimum (restricted) level of retained earnings." (1990: 52).

Leuz, Keller and Stubenrath (1998: 122 et seq.) analyze dividend constraints in debt covenants in Germany. In contrast to the US, German external capital is usually bank debt. As bank debt contracts are not accessible, an analysis of debt covenants is more difficult for Germany. Therefore, Leuz, Keller and Stubenrath interview eight banks to survey if dividend constraints are included in German bank debt contracts.

	Sample Period	Sample Size	Percentage of Firms with Direct Payout Restrictions
Smith, Warner (1979)	1974-1975	87	23%
Castle (1980)		37	62%
Kalay (1982)	1956-1975	150	90%
McDaniel (1986)		92	35%
El Gazzar, Lilien, Pastena (1989)	1970-1981	43	58%
Duke, Hunt (1990)	1984-1985	187	55%
El Gazzar, Pastena (1990)	1970-1982	74	80%
Press, Weintrop (1990)	1985	83	61%
El Gazzar, Pastena (1991)	1976-1982	73	74%
Mohrman (1991)	1977	83	49%
Mohrman (1996)	1963-1990	228	54%
Crawford, Franz, Lobo (2005)	1994-1996	68	59%

Table 5: Payout Restrictions in Debt Covenants in the US, own illustration according to Crawford/Franz/Logo (2005: 533 et seq.) and Leuz/Keller/Stubenrath (1998: 116).

They find that no bank in their sample uses direct dividend constraints. Indirect constraints appear "...only in the context of, for instance, management buy-outs, structured and project financing or when the borrower has a low credit rating, but not in their standard debt agreements." (1998: 122). Furthermore, the study reveals that banks consider the legal constraints in Germany to be strict enough. Therefore, German debt covenants often include other obligations such as collateral (1998: 123).

Besides the analysis of bank debt, a sample of 17 public debt issues (bonds) of German firms are analyzed by Leuz, Keller and Stubenrath (1998: 123 et seq.). They show that in this sample only two bonds have accounting-based restrictions. Unfortunately, the study does not reveal if these financial ratios would be affected by stock dividends.

As illustrated in *Chapter II.2.a*, stock dividends in Germany can impede equity issuances. From this, further costs of false signaling are imposed.

To summarize the insights which literature provides, the retained earnings hypothesis is still unsettled for the US as controversy continues to surround the costs of false signaling. For the German market, it is clear that costs of false signaling exist for stock dividends. In any case, it is disputable whether these costs are high enough.

III.1.b.2.2 Reputation of the Management

Referring to Heinkel (1984), Grinblatt, Masulis and Titman mention the loss of management's reputation after sending a false signal as a further a cost of false signaling (1984: 464). This theory is supported by Penman (1983) who detects information content in managers' earnings forecasts.

A necessary condition for the reputation loss hypothesis is that investors are able to realize which managers signaled correctly and which did not. This might be difficult as an ex-post forecast which shows up to be wrong might have been correct ex-ante.

Another necessary condition of the reputation loss hypothesis is that the market participants agree on which actions are used to signal positive private information. Generally, the risk of reputation loss pressures managers to tell the truth, but the false signal itself does not need to incur further costs. Thus, not only stock dividends but also stock splits could be used as a signal for positive private information from management as long as market participants agree on stock splits as a valid signal for positive prospects. Furthermore, stock splits are a highly appropriate instrument to reveal information as other effects on the firm are comparatively low and the signaling effect of stock splits is less diluted as a result.

III.1.b.2.3 Neglected Firm

Merton's neglected firm hypothesis (1987) claims that transactions such as stock distributions put firms in the spotlight of investors. This hypothesis is of particular relevancy to small (neglected) firms. The presence in the newspapers would reduce the information costs and thus lead to a positive market reaction. In addition, the neglected firm hypothesis leads to a self-selection signal as the splitting firm would be reassessed due to the increased investors' attention. As only managers of undervalued firms like to be reassessed, managers of overestimated firms would try to draw as little attention as possible by forgoing stock distributions (Grinblatt, Masulis, Titman, 1984: 464).

Brennan and Hughes (1991) assume that the neglected firm hypothesis is stronger for stock distributions than for other activities which enhance the firm's advertence. Due to the structure of provisions, firms with high stock prices are less attractive to investors (see *Chapters III.1.b.2.4* and *III.1.c.1*). Therefore, Brennan and Hughes (1991: 1665) argue that analysts neglect firms when share prices are too high. Consequently, managers can increase analysts' attention by reducing their share price by stock distributions. As the neglected firm hypothesis postulates, they will only do so when the stock is undervalued from their perspective.

The validity of the neglected firm hypothesis is questionable when reverse splits are taken into account. If the positive abnormal returns were only based on lower information cost and adverse selection, the same effect should occur for firms which announce reverse splits. In fact, research finds negative abnormal returns following the announcement of reverse splits (Woolridge/Chambers, 1983, Desai/Jain, 1997).

III.1.b.2.4 Trading Range as a Signal

The trading range hypothesis claims that there is an optimal band for stock prices (Copeland, 1979: 115 et seq.). This hypothesis is based on the US provision structure for stock trades (see *Chapter III.1.c.1*). But as Grinblatt, Masulis and Titman (1984: 464 et seq.) and Brennan and Copeland (1988b) claim, the decision for a stock split might also reveal a self-selecting signal. Managers who decrease stock prices by stock distributions near or even below the lower boundary can signal that they expect that the actual stock price will not decline. The costs of false signaling, then, are high transaction costs which occur for low stock prices (see *Chapter III.1.c.1*).

III.1.c Liquidity and Further Explanations

III.1.c.1 Trading Range Hypothesis

The trading range hypothesis postulates that there is an optimal price band in which share prices should be traded (Copeland, 1979)[9]. If share prices are too high, the divisibility of the stock becomes impaired and hence liquidity declines. As Amihud and Mendelson (1986) identify, when positive effects of liquidity on share prices are present, managers should avoid high stock prices by using stock distributions.

Following the liquidity argument of Copeland (1979: 115 et seq.), the stock price should be as low as possible to enhance the divisibility. However, the US brokerage provisions set a lower boundary for optimal stock prices. Provisions in the US usually depend on two factors: the total amount traded and the number of shares. Thus, low share prices lead to a high number of shares traded and thereby to high transaction costs. An illustration of provisions in dependence of share prices can be found in Brennan/Copeland (1988b: 90) and Brennan/Hughes (1991: 1669).

Thus, the trade off between low transaction costs and a high liquidity takes place within the optimal trading range. Since the trading range hy-

[9] See also Grinblatt/Masulis/Titmann (1984), Lakonishok/Lev (1987), Brennan/Copeland (1988), McNichols/Dravid (1990).

pothesis neglects the accounting method, the theory holds for both, stock splits and stock dividends.

The consideration that high stock prices negatively affect liquidity can be applied to the German market as well. But for Germany, the lower boundary cannot be explained by the provision structure since German provisions are a linear function over the value of the transaction (Kaserer/Brunner, 1997: 79). Gebhardt, Entrup and Heiden state that a lower boundary of the trading range might arise from the restrictions which occur for new equity issuances (1994: 315) when the stock price is too close to the par value (see *Chapter II.2.a*). Additionally, the ability of firms to split stock is generally limited by the minimum par value for stock splits. For stock dividends, firms can only issue bonus shares to lower the stock price as long as they have enough available funds which can be reallocated into capital stock and they are willing to reduce distributable funds. From there, further lower boundaries for stock prices arise in Germany.

III.1.c.2 Further Explanations

Literature provides further explanations for the positive market reaction on the announcement of stock dividends.

When capital stock is reduced, creditor protection rules have to be satisfied (see *Chapter II.2.b*). Thus, a reallocation of distributable funds to capital stock leads to a credit enhancement while the risk that liable equity is withdrawn at the expense of creditors declines. (Kaserer/Brunner, 1997: 80). As a result, costs of debt may decline. Assuming goal congruence between managers and shareholders, managers would then only increase capital stock as long as the gains of lower costs of external capital exceed the disadvantages from the reduction of distributable funds. Hence the market value of equity increases when stock dividends are announced.

While capital stock generally secures creditors' claims, Burghof (1998) finds that under certain assumptions the opposite is the case for distressed firms wherein capital stock protects shareholders from creditors. The two main assumptions are that first, creditors have control over the restructuring and second, equity needs to be issued after the restructuring.

When creditors decide on an investment plan, they logically do not maximize the firms' total value or equity value, but rather the value of debt. Consequentially, creditors will implement an investment plan in which redemption of debt is most likely. In doing so, positive net present value projects might be rejected at the expense of the shareholders.

But after the specification of the investment plan equity needs to be issued, the issuance will fail when the market value of equity for the given investment plan is lower than the issuance price. Since share price for equity issues may not be lower than the par value (see *Chapter II.2.a*), high par values may force creditors to account for shareholders' interests when restructuring distressed firms.

Bechmann and Raaballe (2007: 590) find that stock splits are purely cosmetic events, thereby conflicting with the assumption that investment decisions are made rationally.

III.1.d Jensen's Free Cash Flow Hypothesis

A fair number of studies investigate the stock market impact of stock distributions. Since none of the studies finds negative abnormal returns, theory focuses on the positive effects of stock distributions. Even though Kaserer/Brunner (1997: 80) take into consideration that stock dividends might be disadvantageous for shareholders as distribution of funds are aggravated, negative effects of stock dividends have yet to be investigated.

Negative effects can be revealed by analyzing stock dividends against the background of Jensen's free cash flow hypothesis (1986). Jensen defines free cash flow as the cash flow that remains after all positive net present value projects are financed. Managers of firms with a high free cash flow have incentives for over-investment. In these cases, managers could use stock dividends to further deprive capital from the shareholders by transferring retained earnings to capital stock. As this consideration is only relevant for firms that account for the stock distributions, the free cash flow hypothesis is only significant for stock dividends, not for stock splits. Thus, the stock market impact for firms with high free cash flow should be lower than for other firms. The free cash flow hypothesis will be analyzed empirically in *Chapter V.2*.

III.1.e Conclusions

The two main explanations for the positive stock market reaction to the announcement of stock distributions are signaling and liquidity effects. Regarding the costs of false signaling, the following theories can be applied to stock distributions: the reputation loss of management, the neglected firm hypothesis and the lower boundary of the optimal trading range.

Following the retained earnings hypothesis, for stock dividends, further costs of false signaling arise from the accounting treatment. In literature, the retained earnings hypothesis is the most common signaling approach for stock distributions. Hence, stock dividends are more likely to convey information than stock splits do.

All other signaling and liquidity-based explanations can similarly demonstrate the positive market reactions for both stock splits and stock dividends. However, literature describes a coexistence of all effects as most likely. The following chapter will describe and discuss empirical evidence for these theories.

III.2 Empirical Evidence

III.2.a Evidence from the US

III.2.a.1 Signaling Effects

Stock distributions in the US have been a topic of numerous studies and have a long history in research. Multiple studies investigate stock distributions in the US, analyzing the general stock price impact, the validity of signaling and liquidity-based theories, risk effects of stock distributions and the stock market response on the ex-day. This chapter summarizes the main empirical findings literature provides for the US.

MacKinlay references what may be the first event study ever that analyzes stock distributions (1997: 13). These early studies by Dolley (1933a, 1933b) reveal that in his sample of stock splits, returns on the ex-day are prevalently positive.

Several subsequent studies by Myers/Bakay (1948), Barker (1956, 1957) and Johnson (1966) investigate stock market returns surrounding the ex-day of stock distributions. All of them find that returns are positive before the ex-day. By far, the most cited empirical study of stock distributions is the paper by Fama et al. (1969), as it started a "methodological revolution" of event studies (Binder, 1998: 111). Based on Fama et al. (1969), literature has developed a broad variety of empirical analysis of stock distributions. The following chapters provide an overview and discussion of the most relevant studies for the US market.

Unfortunately, when investigating the role of the accounting treatment, major studies do not differ appropriately for the accounting method. While the classification is clear cut in Germany (Wulff, 2002: 54), Rankine and Stice find in their study (*1997B: 161 et seq.*) that in the US, the distinction of stock splits, small stock dividends and large stock dividends is frequently inaccurate.

Within their sample of 337 stock distributions, 77 percent of the classifications of the Center of Research on Security Prices (CRSP) are incorrect[10]. As a result, the impact of the accounting method which relies on the qualification of the CRSP (among them Grinblatt/Masulis/Titmann, 1984, Lakonishok/Lev, 1987, Brennan/Copeland, 1988b, Asquith/Healy/Palepu, 1989, McNichols/Dravid, 1990, Brennan/Hughes, 1991, Arbel/Swanson, 1993 and Peterson/Millar/Rimbey, 1996) is biased. Other studies such as Fama et al. (1969), classify all stock distributions with more than 25 percent of new shares as stock splits, ignoring large stock dividends altogether (see *Chapter II.1.a*).

But the ex-post classification by the CRSP is not the only one that is biased. In the announcement of the firm, managers describe the accounting method incorrectly in 30 percent of the sample (Rankine/Stice, 1997B: 180). For the purposes of analyzing the impact of the accounting method, CRSP's incorrect classification is not a crucial issue as one might collect data about stock dividend announcements elsewhere. But if already the announcements are classified incorrectly, investigations on the stock price effect of the accounting method are aggravated. The error ratio of the announcements is so high that investors take into account the possibility that the firms' classification may be wrong for each announcement.

---

[10] Data concerning the classification of stock distributions from other sources, such as the S&P Dividend Record, The Wall Street Journal and Moody's Dividend Record are strongly biased as well. An overview can be found in the study by Rankine and Stice (1997B: 168).

Confusing the characteristics of stock splits and stock distributions is not exclusive to managers and the CRSP. Foster III and Scribner (1998) analyze the coverage of stock splits and stock dividends of eight accounting textbooks between 1994 and 1995. They conclude "It is intended to help accounting educators provide a more informed coverage of generally accepted accounting principles for stock distributions than is available in current textbook." (1998: 9). Hence, it is difficult to figure out the true impact of the accounting method by using US data.

The first empirical evidence for signaling effects was delivered by Fama et al. (1969). They find that stock distributions are frequently followed by increases in cash dividends. After the ex-day, stock prices of dividend-increasing firms stay high, while stock prices decline for firms that reduce dividends. Fama et al. therefore conclude that the positive effects of stock distributions on share prices primarily result from investors' expectations that dividends will be increased.

Grinblatt, Masulis and Titman (1984) support the findings of Fama et al. that stock distributions are positively correlated with dividend increases. Going a step further they show that stock dividends have higher abnormal returns than stock splits. Assuming that the accounting method is the main or the only difference between stock splits and stock dividends, the higher returns of stock dividends provide evidence for the retained earnings hypothesis.

The studies by McNichols, Dravid (1986), Lakonishok, Lev (1987) and Rankine, Stice (1997b) provide further evidence that stock distributions convey managers' private information. McNichols, Dravid (1986) detect an increase of earnings after the distribution and find a positive correlation between the split ratio and earnings forecasts errors. Lakonishok, Lev (1987) compare splitting firms with non-splitting firms. They find that earnings growth is higher for those that split.

In contrast, Asquith, Healy and Palepu (1989) observe no near-term cash dividend increase or increase in earnings after the announcement of stock splits. Asquith, Healy and Palepu find that earnings have already increased before the announcement of a split. They believe that stock splits can signal that earnings increases are not temporary but permanent.

A more differentiated analysis of cash dividend development after the announcement of stock distributions has been done by Rankine and Stice (1997a). They also show that dividend growth after the announcement is significantly higher for firms that reduced retained earnings substantially. Furthermore, Rankine and Stice detect a significant positive correlation between the relative amount of retained earnings transferred into capital stock and abnormal returns in the announcement period.

In a different study, Rankine/Stice (1997b) compare abnormal returns from the announcements of stock splits and stock dividends. Consistent with Grinblatt, Masulis and Titman (1984), they find that abnormal returns are higher for stock dividends than for stock splits. Within the group of stock dividends, abnormal returns are higher first for firms which incorporate in more restrictive states (see *Chapter II.2.b*) and second for firms which have low retained earnings prior to the stock dividend. Furthermore, Rankine and Stice (1997b) identify a positive correlation between the abnormal returns in the announcement period and earnings change for stock dividends (1997b: 180). In contrast, abnormal returns from stock splits are not correlated with earnings changes.

An analysis of the abnormal returns in dependency of legal payout restrictions which arise from stock dividends is also done by Peterson/Millar/Rimbey (1996). They come to the same conclusion as Rankine/Stice (1997b) that abnormal returns are significantly higher for those firms which reduce distributable funds (1996: 249).

Besides the strong evidence for signaling effects of stock distributions generally and in particular for the retained earnings hypothesis for stock dividends, Crawford, Franz and Lobo (2005) dispute the prominence of the retained earnings hypothesis in the US. They reason that the costs of false signaling caused by the accounting method are rather small for the majority of firms (2005: 561, see also *Chapters II.2.b* and *III.1.b.2.1*).

To find empirical evidence, Crawford, Franz and Lobo replicate the analysis of Rankine/Stice (1997a, 1997b). In the study of 1997a the regression model is modified and one outlier is deleted (543 et seq.). For the study of 1997b they find that the results are biased due to incorrect announcement dates provided by CRSP. After correcting the announcement days, abnormal returns are not dependent on the accounting method anymore for most of the firms. (2005: 553 et seqq.).

Finally, Crawford, Lobo and Franz state that empirical evidence of the retained earnings hypothesis is restricted to firms that are incorporated in states with restrictive regulation of cash dividends (see *Chapter II.2.b*). As this is the case only for a small number of firms, they conclude that "...evidence no longer supports the retained earnings hypothesis for the general population of publicly traded companies." (2005: 561).

To find evidence for the signaling theory, Mohanty/Moon (2007) compare abnormal returns of firms that are likely to have high information asymmetry with those that have low information asymmetry. Signaling effects should weigh heavier for high information asymmetry firms and the abnormal returns should be higher as a result. In a first test, they assume that depository institutions face lower information asymmetry than industrial firms. In a second test, firms with high research and development activities are assumed to have high information asymmetry. For both tests, Mohanty and Moon find no difference between abnormal returns of high- and low-information asymmetry firms. Therefore, they contradict the signaling theory.

As Mohanty and Moon investigate stock splits, it is still questionable if evidence for the signaling theory could be found for stock dividends in states with restrictive dividend statutes.

Beside the retained earnings hypothesis, Arbel/Swanson (1993) offer further evidence for the signaling theory by citing the neglected firm hypothesis. Trying to eliminate contamination by other news, they first delete firms from their sample which released other information like dividend announcements, earnings forecasts or share repurchases within the announcement period (1993: 17). On the announcement day and the following day, they find evidence that stock prices react stronger when firms are covered only by few for no analysts (1993: 20, 26). However, since analysts' coverage is positively correlated with the size of the firm (Bhushan, 1989: 261 et seq.), it is questionable whether the higher returns for the subsamples are in fact caused by analysts' coverage or by other size effects.

Brennan/Hughes (1991) reason that firms with high stock prices are less attractive for trading due to the provision structure and therefore attract less analyst interest (see *Chapter III.1.b.2.3*). After controlling for size and other effects, they still discover a negative correlation between the price prior to the distribution and the number of analysts (1991: 1682 et seqq.). This leads to a self-selection of good firms to distribute stocks, as only managers with positive private information are willing to draw the attraction of analysts to their company.

III.2.a.2 Liquidity Effects

Several studies cite evidence for the trading range hypothesis, observing positive abnormal returns corresponding to high firm-specific stock prices prior to the announcement (Fama et al., 1969, Grinblatt/Masulis/Titman (1984), Asquith/Healey/Palepu (1989), Lakonishok/Lev (1987), McNichols/Dravid (1990), Maloney/Mulherin (1992), Mohanty/Moon (2007)). The high stock returns before the announcement indicate that the stock prices might have exceeded the upper boundary of the optimal trading range and therefore, management might have considered that a stock distribution is required to return the stock price to the trading range. This is in consensus with Crawford, Franz, Lobo (2005: 560) who find that abnormal returns and split ratios correlate with the share price before distribution. Fama et al. detect that the number of stock distributions increases enormously in years when stock prices are generally high (1969: 11 et seq.).

Other studies analyze the liquidity effects of stock distributions to find evidence for the trading range hypothesis. Following this theory, liquidity should increase after the stock distribution due to a better divisibility and lower brokerage fees. Following the theory of efficient markets (Fama, 1970, 1991, see also *Chapter IV.2.a*), the additional value of equity on account of the higher liquidity is anticipated in stock prices immediately upon the announcement. Nevertheless, the direct effect on liquidity cannot be anticipated and thus will not occur before the ex-day. Literature uses different measures for liquidity to analyze changes in liquidity caused by stock distributions. However, empirical evidence concerning liquidity effects is mixed and puzzling. Harrison (2000: 74 et seqq.) gives a comprehensive overview of literature. Subsequently, essential findings will be highlighted.

Studies by Copeland (1979), Murray (1985), Lakonishok/Lev (1987), Lamoureux/Poon (1987) and Maloney/Mulherin (1992) investigate changes in the trading volume. With respect to volume, all of those studies find a decrease after stock distributions. While Copeland (1979) detects that the negative volume change begins before the announcement, the other studies find increases in liquidity in this period. Fewer studies by Dolley (1933a, 1933b) and Mohanty/Moon (2007) detect a significant increase in trading volume immediately following the announcement day.

In addition, Copeland (1979), Murray (1985) and Maloney/Mulherin (1992) state that the bid-ask spreads increase after stock distribution. Analogous to this result, Han (1995) finds opposite effects for reverse splits which lead to increases in trading volume and the bid-ask spread declines. The higher bid-ask spread after stock distributions not only contradicts the trading range hypothesis. The bid-ask spread can also be used as a measure for information asymmetry (Bhattacharya/Daouk, 2002: 76). Following the signaling theory, the degree of information asymmetry should decline after information is revealed by stock distributions. Therefore, the increase of bid-ask spreads queries both, liquidity and signaling effects.

While analyzing trading volume and bid-ask spreads undermines the hypothesis that stock distributions increase liquidity, other studies still find evidence of the trading range hypothesis. Lamoureux/Poon (1987) and Maloney/Mulherin (1992) additionally investigate the changes in shareholders structure and both find an increase in the number of shareholders. However, Powell/Baker (1993) do not support these findings but instead detect a shift from private to institutional shareholders. Likewise, Maloney/Mulherin observe that the increase in the number of shareholders in their study is above average for institutional investors (1992: 55).

A completely different approach to measure liquidity effects is pursued by Muscarella and Vetsuypens (1996). They analyze the effect of the splits of American Depository Receipts (ADR) when only the ADR and not the underlying stock is split. By analyzing ADRs, they can exclude any signaling effects which are attributed to stock distributions. Still, they find positive abnormal returns in the announcement period for the ADRs and therefore provide strong evidence for the liquidity hypothesis (1996: 24).

III.2.b Evidence from Germany

III.2.b.1 General Findings

Several studies approve the US results for the German market and find positive abnormal returns when firms announce stock distributions.

Schulz (1972) analyzes the impact of stock dividends on stock prices for the German market with a sample of 31 breweries, comparing the chart of firms that announced stock dividends with the industry index. Schulz finds positive abnormal returns and detects a positive correlation to the split ratio. Furthermore, he detects positive abnormal returns several months before the announcement day. He reasons that the early abnormal returns are caused by insider trading (Schulz, 1972: 148 et seqq.). However, the early positive abnormal returns may be due to tardy estimated announcement dates for some companies in the sample (1972: 161). Unfortunately, no tests of significance are applied to the findings. The study is solely descriptive and does not investigate the reasons for the positive effects of stock dividends on stock prices.

Harrison analyzes the motivation for stock splits (115 et seqq.). He interprets the results from 54 questionnaires on split shares between 1995 and 1997 after the minimum par value was reduced from 50 DM to 5 DM in the summer of 1994. The objective of the study is stock splits and evidence for stock distribution is provided.

All 54 firms state that one reason for the split is to make the share more attractive to investors. The following most common reasons are also related to the enhancement of marketability. They are: a lower share price, a share price closer to industry average, optimal trading range, a higher number of shareholders, an increase of liquidity and the practicability of equity issuances[11]. Since liquidity effects play a decisive role, it is puzzling that 59 percent of the companies do not expect that the market value will be increased by the stock split. It is curious, then, why managers try to increase liquidity.

Furthermore, only 33 percent of the firms believe that investor advertence is not increased by stock splits. Following the neglected firm hypothesis (see *Chapter III.1.b.2.3*), a self-selection process, then, should have the result that only mangers with positive private information split their stock. However, only 18.5 percent of the companies assume that stock splits reveal information about firms' prospects to the market.

As discussed in *Chapter II.1.c*, German stock is usually traded at minimum par value. For this reason, stock splits are prohibited for a vast majority of companies unless the legislature lowers the minimum par value.

---

[11] As discussed in *Chapter III.1.c.2*, the greater practicability of future equity issuances has no relation on the changes of par value. Therefore, it can be assumed that managers represent the advantage of future equity issuances to greater marketability.

As a consequence, companies and lobbyists encouraged lowering of the minimum par value in 1993. Most touted the advantages of a lower par value as well as the resulting liberalization of stock splits which could be subsumed under enhancement of marketability (Harrison (2000: 40 et seq.). Hence, the findings of Harrison's (2000) questionnaire are supported by lobbyists' statements. Companies and lobbyists believe in addition to this, though, that the market value of equity might be increased by stock splits.

The accounting method of stock distributions in Germany is clear cut and, in contrast to the US, independent from the split ratio (see *Chapter II.1.a*). Assuming, that managers who want to reduce their share price want to incur as few other effects as possible, they would prefer stock splits over stock dividends. Consequently, the only motivation to choose a stock dividend instead of a stock split should lie in the intended effects of the accounting method. However, since stock splits are typically not allowed due to par values, stock dividends are the only way for many firms to reduce the share price[12]. Therefore, not all stock dividends can be assumed to be primarily motivated by accounting effects. Thus, marketability increase as a motivation for stock splits is also applicable to stock dividends when stock splits are prohibited.

While a multitude of studies investigate stock distribution in the US, only a few studies exist as regards the German market. An overview over the most important studies is outlined in *Table 6*. *Table 6* highlights the fact that in Germany, like in the US (see *Chapter III.2.a.1*), abnormal returns in the announcement period are higher for stock dividends than for stock splits. For stock splits, only weak evidence is found to support a positive price reaction. Further insights that literature provides for stock distribution will be discussed in the following sections.

---

[12] Stock dividends have no direct effect on liquidity when no bonus shares are issued (see *Chapter II.1.c*).

Study	Event	Sample Period	Sample Size	Model	Abnormal Returns		Significance
Padberg (1995)	Stock Dividends	1972 - 1991	121	Market Model	[0]	1.84%	***
					[-1; 0]	2.52%	not tested
					[+3; +15]	0.15%	not tested
					[-15; -2]	2.48%	not tested
					[-15; +15]	6.64%	not tested
Gebhardt/Entrup/Heiden (1994)	Stock Dividends	1980 - 1990	55	Market Model	[0]	2.47%	***
					[-1; 0]	3.51%	***
					[+2; +30]	-0.37%	not tested
					[-30; -3]	3.20%	not tested
					[-30; +30]	6.46%	not tested
Kaserer/Brunner (1997)	Stock Dividends	1962 - 1991	181	Market Model	[0]	2.19%	***
					[-1; 0]	2.81%	***
					[0; +1]	3.60%	***
					[0; +5]	4.35%	***
					[-5; 0]	3.57%	***
					[-30; +30]	9.50%	***
					[-250; +250]	19.38%	***
Harrison (2000)	Stock Splits	1994 - 1997	137	Market Model	[0]	0.00%	
					[-5; -1]	0.61%	*
					[+1; +5]	-0.17%	
Wulff (2001)	Stock Splits	1994 - 1996	78	Market Model	[0]	0.01%	
					[-1]	-0.15%	
					[+1]	0.47%	***
					[-10; +10]	1.76%	not tested

Table 6: Abnormal Returns at the Announcement of Stock Distributions in Germany.

III.2.b.2 Signaling Effects

Since abnormal returns are higher for stock dividends than for stock splits (see *Table 6*), it can be presumed that the accounting treatment of stock dividends has positive effects on the market value of equity. Nevertheless, Gebhardt/Entrup/Heiden (1994: 315) note that the retained earnings hypothesis cannot always be applied to German stock dividends. They reason that distributable funds are only reduced when retained earnings, not capital reserves or legal reserves, are reallocated in capital stock. However, as discussed in *Chapter II.2.b*, distributable funds are indirectly reduced at the minimum even if capital stock is increased from capital reserves or legal reserves. Furthermore, in 83 percent of the stock dividends (Gebhardt/Entrup/Heiden, 1994: 311), retained earnings and not capital reserves are reduced. In further consideration, then, it will be assumed that stock dividends generally have an impact on distributable funds.

Evidence for signaling effects is given by Gebhardt/Entrup/Heiden (1994), Padberg (1995), Kaserer/Brunner (1997), and Wulff (2001, 2002) for the German market. The relevant results of these studies will be discussed in this section.

Gebhardt/Entrup/Heiden (1994) and Kaserer/Brunner (1997) show that firms that announce stock dividends and equity issues at the same time have lower abnormal returns than firms that announce a stock dividend only (1994: 322 et seq.). But even for the firms that simultaneously announce an equity issue, the abnormal returns remain significantly positive. Gebhardt/Entrup/Heiden (1994: 322) reason that abnormal returns are smaller for firms that simultaneously announce an equity issue as they obviously are not able to finance high future dividends by future earnings of existing investments.

Gebhardt/Entrup/Heiden (1994) find that abnormal returns are especially high for companies when retained earnings divided by dividends paid are smaller after the split (Gebhardt/Entrup/Heiden 1994: 325). Since the effect is not stastically significant, these findings provide only slight additional evidence for the retained earnings hypothesis in Germany.

Stronger evidence for the retained earnings hypothesis emerges from the investigation of post-announcement dividend changes. Gebhardt/Entrup/Heiden (1994: 314) observe that 64 of 69 stock dividend announcements are followed by dividend increases in the same year. In the two years after the stock dividend, only 9 of the 69 companies reduced dividends. Likewise, Kaserer/Brunner (1997: 92) find only 5 firms out of 181 that reduced their cash distributions to shareholders after a stock dividend.

Kaserer/Brunner (1997) find high cumulative abnormal returns of 8.99 percent prior to the announcement in the period [-250; -6] (see *Table 7*). Since firms naturally tend to issue stock dividends in times when the company is attractable to investors, the effect of stock price as a result of the stock dividend announcement could be diluted (1997: 89). To account for this, Kaserer/Brunner independently investigate companies that issue stock dividends repeatedly over time. They assume that these companies issue stock dividends independently from prior stock market returns. This is affirmed by the significantly lower cumulative abnormal returns of 3.74 percent in the pre-announcement period [-250; -6]. However, the cumulative abnormal returns in the announcement period [-2; 0] are equal as *Table 7* shows. Since abnormal returns are independent from pre-announcement abnormal returns, Kaserer/Brunner reason that announcements of stock dividends convey additional positive information to investors (1997: 91).

	All Stock Dividends	**Singular Stock Dividends**	**Repeated Stock Dividends**
[-250; -6]	8.99%	11.22%	3.74%
[-2-, 0]	2.97%	2.98%	2.93%

Table 7: Cumulative Abnormal Returns of Singular and Repeated Stock Dividends (Kaserer/Brunner, 1997: 85, 91).

Padberg (1995: 256 et seqq.) compares the abnormal returns of the financial and non-financial sector. While non-financial companies' cumulative abnormal returns in the period [-15; +15] are 7 percent, the cumulative abnormal returns of financial institutions are only 4 percent (1995: 267). Padberg argues that in the financial sector, stock dividends are issued independently from the prospects of the institute and therefore, the signaling effect is less strong. Another explanation is given by Mohanty/Moon (2007: 980 et seq., see also *Chapter III.2.a.1*). In their study for the US market, they argue that signaling effects of stock dividends are lower for financial institutions since information asymmetry is lower in the financial sector due to regulation and supervision.

Gebhardt/Entrup/Heiden (1994) and Wulff (2002) investigate the neglected firm hypothesis. Since small firms are more likely to be neglected by investors and analysts (Bhushan, 1989: 261 et seq., see also *Chapter III.2.a.1*), they set forth to analyze the relationship of the firm size[13] and cumulative abnormal returns. Gebhardt/Entrup/Heiden divide their sample in small, medium and large firms. They find that in the period [-1; 0], large firms have significantly smaller abnormal returns than small- and medium-sized firms (1994: 324). Wulff (2002: 292 et seqq.) approves these findings by a cross-sectional analysis. He finds evidence that the cumulative abnormal returns are a linear decreasing function of firm size.

Kaserer/Brunner (1997: 92 et seqq.) find additional evidence for signaling effects by investigating the abnormal returns in dependency of the split ratio. They find a significant positive relationship between the percentaged increase of shares corresponding to capital stock and abnormal returns. This first result indicates that the stock price effect of stock distributions cannot be explained by the neglected firm or reputation loss hypothesis alone. Furthermore, Kaserer/Brunner argue that firms generally try to keep dividends per share constant after a stock dividend and therefore the total cash distribution increases. In Germany, new shares can be excluded from dividend payments in the year of the split (§ 217 II AktG). Investigating firms separately which exercise this option reveals that the explanatory power of the split ratio for cumulative abnormal returns is extraordinarily high. Kaserer/Brunner reason that in this context, investors interpret the split ratio as a signal for the subsequent year's increase of cash distributions.

[13] Both studies, Gebhardt/Entrup/Heiden (1994) and Wulff (2002), define firm size by the market value of equity.

III.2.b.3 Liquidity Effects

The findings of Kaserer/Brunner (1997:92 et seqq.) that the cumulative abnormal returns increase with the proportion of new shares issued can also be interpreted as support for the liquidity hypothesis. The lower the split ratio (the higher the increase of the number of shares), the more substantially the stock price is reduced and the positive liquidity effects should be more pronounced.

Harrison doubts that liquidity is increased by stock distributions (2000: 252). Analyzing the changes of bid-ask spreads after the exday, Harrison even finds an increase of the bid-ask spread and thus a reduction of liquidity (2000. 241 et seqq.). However, this change is not statistically significant.

In contrast, Wulff (2001: 209 et seq., 2002), using other measures for liquidity, finds strong evidence for an increase in liquidity after the exday of stock distributions. He detects a significant reduction of days without any trade after stock splits between 1974 and 1996. The average volume turnover is significantly increased as well[14]. In contrast, the mean split-adjusted volume slightly declines. This can be explained by outliers, since the median is significantly increased by 90.24 percent.

However, the extent of the liquidity effect has no influence on the level of cumulative abnormal returns as Wulff (2002) shows. In a cross-sectional analysis, he finds no significant relationship between cumulative abnormal returns and changes in the above mentioned liquidity measures volume, volume turnover and percentage of days with trade (2002: 293).

Wulff concludes: "Despite a substantial increase in liquidity after the split, I cannot find support for the liquidity hypothesis. Improved liquidity seems not to be valued by market participants in Germany." (2002: 294). These findings are supported by the results of Kaserer/Brunner (1997, see *Table 7*). The fact that stock dividends are usually issued after high abnormal returns suggests that the share price might have exceeded the upper boundary of the optimal trading range and as a consequence, managers want to reduce the share price by stock distributions in order to

[14] Volume is defined as the split-adjusted number of traded shares. Volume turnover is the non-split-adjusted number of traded shares relative to the number of shares outstanding (Wulff (2002: 292).

increase liquidity. However, consistent with the results of Wulff (2001, 2002), the cumulative abnormal returns for stock dividends are independent from those abnormal returns prior to the announcement (Kaserer/Brunner, 1997: 91).

Previous studies do not mention that the abnormal returns in the announcement period might have been caused by an earlier anticipation of stock splits. As discussed in *Chapter II.1.c*, the par value of German companies is usually at the minimum par value. When the minimum par value is lowered, the par value of the companies converge to the new minimum par value. When investors are aware of this process, they will anticipate a general increase of stock splits as early as when the information emerges and that the minimum par value will be lowered. This theory is in accordance with the main empirical findings for German stock splits as follows:

1. the positive abnormal returns prior to the announcement,
2. the merely marginal abnormal returns in the announcement period and
3. the increase of liquidity after the ex-day.

These findings unravel the puzzle as to why liquidity is increased after the ex-day while stock prices only marginally react to the announcement as the valuation of higher liquidity was already incorporated in the share price.

Since reductions of the minimum par value are usually claimed and discussed publicly (Harrison, 2000: 32 et seqq.), information about changes in regulation are revealed gradually. It is difficult, then, to investigate the impact of reductions of the minimum par value on stock markets.

While stock splits can be anticipated when the minimum par value is reduced, no such patterns exist for stock dividends. In contrast to stock splits, it is possible that positive liquidity effects for stock dividends are incorporated into the share price in the announcement period.

IV Data and Methodology

IV.1 Descriptive Data

IV.1.a Data Collection

For the purpose of the study, German data is more useful than US data for the following reasons:

1. Investors in Germany can clearly identify the accounting treatment at the time of the announcement. In contrast, there still is confusion among market participants about the accounting method in the US. It has been established that textbooks have not covered this sufficiently. Therefore, managers use the wrong classifications in 30 percent of the announcements (see *Chapter II.1.a*). Consequently, it is doubtful whether managers are capable to use the accounting method specifically to reveal private information. Furthermore, investors cannot separate ex-ante if the accounting method is announced correctly. Thus, they demand a risk premium for unintended signaling and the observed impact of the accounting treatment on abnormal returns declines.
2. In Germany, all firms are exposed to equal legal dividend constraints by the federal stock corporation act. Theoretical and empirical evidence supports that the accounting treatment of stock dividends in Germany reduces distributable funds. In contrast, for US firms theoretical and empirical investigations about the relevance of the accounting treatment is controversial. Literature suggests that the retained earnings hypothesis is only applicable to a small number of US firms (see *Chapter III*).

To identify the firms that announced stock dividends in Germany, data is collected from Datastream. The sample includes 212 announcements of stock dividends from March 1991 to May 2006. The announcement day is the first day on which a stock dividend appears on LexisNexis. Most announcements first appeared in the Börsenzeitung, VWD and the Frankfurter Allgemeine Zeitung. As LexisNexis does not contain all media, the announcements dates in our sample might be too late as other media might have spread information earlier.

The total sample size is reduced to 192 because either the announcement date could not be identified[15] or the data was not available. A list of the firms in the sample can be found in *Appendix 2*.

IV.1.b Size of the Firms

Three measures for the size of the firms are regarded: market value of common equity, total assets and total sales. To exclude the effects of the stock dividend, the values of the year prior to the announcement are collected for each firm. The sample contains all sizes of firms starting at a market value of 1.6 million Euro and ending at the highest market value of 84,253.2 million Euro. In the case of all three measures, the median is lower than the mean; there is a high number of small firms and some outliers at the upper end. A detailed overview over the sizes of the firms in the sample is given in *Appendix 3*.

IV.1.c Distributions of Events through Time

With respect to the number of announcements per year, there is a significant increase in the years 1999 and 2000. Bechmann and Raaballe (2007: 582) find that in these years, stock splits have been popular in Denmark as well.

There are two reasons for the high number of announcements in 1999 and 2000. One reason is the introduction of the Euro in January 1999. The conversion of the Deutsche Mark into the Euro led to odd nominal values and managers wanted to take account of that. Twenty-nine of the 87 firms that announced in 1999 and 2000, explicitly gave the introduction of the Euro as a major reason for the stock dividend in this sample.

---

[15] For a few stock dividends, LexisNexis only provides information about the ex-date.

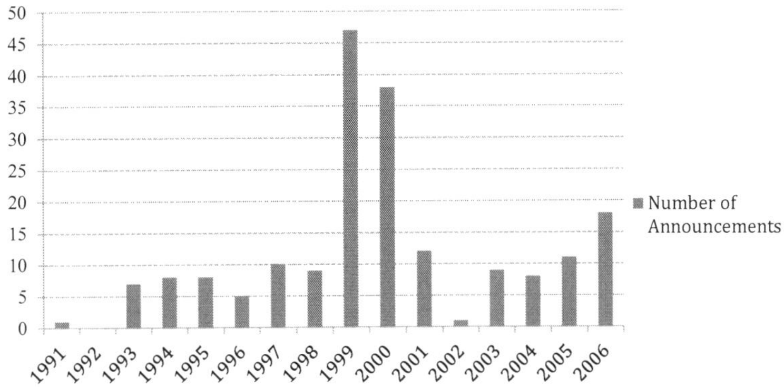

Figure 1: Number of Announcements per Year.

In addition, in 1999 the minimum par value was reduced from 5 DM to 1 Euro. As discussed in *Chapter II.1.c* and *III.2.b*, a reduction of the minimum par value primarily gives the firms a broader latitude for stock splits, not for stock dividends. Hence, a the reduction of the minimum par value should lead to a shift from stock dividends to stock splits, which cannot explain the enormous increase of stock dividends in 1999 and 2000. Besides 1999, the minimum par value was lowered in 1994. In this year, no significant change in the number of stock dividends is detected.

Another explanation can found in the trading range hypothesis. Due to the rapid growth of stock prices between 1997 and 2000, managers might have wanted to reduce the stock price to the optimal trading range by stock splits.

IV.1.d Split Ratio

The average split ratios of different subsamples give a deeper insight in the motivation for the stock dividend. The split ratios are collected from Datastream (capital issues and changes) and are available for 146 firms.

Formula 12:

$$Split\ Ratio = \frac{Number\ of\ Old\ Shares}{Number\ of\ New\ Shares}$$

Table 8 shows the mean split ratios and the number of firms for different subsamples. As one would expect, with 7.09 the mean split ratio of the Euro Converters is on a very high level and as a consequence, the number of new shares compared to the number of old shares is quite low. The reason is that Euro Converters only want to bring the nominal values to an even number. Therefore, they will keep the number of issued shares as low as possible, to keep other effects of stock dividends as low as possible.

	Mean Split Ratio	Number
All	2.42	198
1999-2000	3.81	87
Without 1999-2000	1.36	111
1999-2000 without Euro Converters	2.50	58
Euro Converters	7.09	29
Without Euro Converters	1.76	169

Table 8: Mean Split Ratios of Different Subsamples.

Beyond that, the table shows that the split ratio is not only higher for the Euro Converters that explicitly mentioned the Euro conversion as the motivation for the stock dividend. The rest of the firms that announced in 1999 and 2000 still have a mean split ratio of 2.50, while the mean split ratio in the other years is only 1.36.

The generally high mean split ratio of 3.81 in 1999 and 2000 in comparison to a mean split ratio of 1.36 in the other years indicates that it is unlikely, that the high number of stock dividends in these years are caused by the trading range hypothesis. Following the trading range hypothesis, high stock prices would lead to low split ratios as for the firms, the stocks would then be further above the optimal trading range. As *Table 8* shows, the opposite is the case.

IV.2 Event Study Design

IV.2.a Market Efficiency

The theory of market efficiency by Fama (1970, 1991) is crucial when measuring the content of new information by analysing stock returns (May, 1991: 314). Following this theory, stock prices "fully reflect" all available information. Jensen (1978: 96) finds a general definition of market efficiency: "A market is efficient with respect to information set θ_t, if it is impossible to make economic profits[16] by trading on the basis of information set θ_t.".

Fama distinguishes three forms of market efficiency (1970: 388):

1. Weak form

   All information which can be derived from past prices is incorporated into the stock prices. Stock prices can then be described as a random walk (Fama, 1970: 390).

[16] Economic profits are "risk-adjusted returns net of all costs" (Jensen, 1978: 96).

2. Semi-strong form

   Additionally to 1., all information (such as the announcements of stock distributions) which is available publicly is fully reflected by the stock prices.

3. Strong form

   Additionally to 1. and 2., private information of insiders is fully reflected by the stock prices.

Fama bases this theory on the assumption that no frictions exist on the market (1970: 387):

1. No transaction costs
2. No costs for information
3. Homogenous expectations of all market participants

Padberg (1995: 159) complements a fourth assumption that all market participants decide rationally. Even while these assumptions cannot be satisfied in reality, Fama still believes that market efficiency can exist on capital markets (1970: 388).

This study investigates the impact of stock dividends on the value of equity. The semi-strong form of market efficiency allows for the examination of changes in stock prices to measure the effects of stock dividends on market values. Following Fama (1991: 1575) and Jensen (1978:96), stock prices will react to the announcement of stock dividends as long as the value of the announcement is higher than the frictions on the capital markets, such as transaction costs.

As market efficiency postulates that information is incorporated into the stock price immediately, the effects of stock dividends on the market value of equity are therefore already reflected in the market price at the time of the announcement and not of the execution. As stock dividends need to be approved by the shareholders, there is still uncertainty about whether the stock dividend might fail. For this reason, there still might be additional effects on the market value when the shareholders resolve the stock dividend.

IV.2.b Computation of Abnormal Returns

IV.2.b.1 Discrete and Continuous Returns

Returns can generally be calculated as discrete or as continuous (logarithmic) returns (Röder, 1999: 13 et seq., Strong, 1992 and Dorfleitner, 2002). Discrete returns $r_{i,t}^{discr.}$ are calculated by

Formula 13:

$$r_{i,t}^{discr.} = \frac{P_{i,t} + D_{i,t} - P_{i,t}}{P_{i,t-1}} = \frac{P_{i,t} + D_{i,t}}{P_{i,t-1}} - 1$$

where $P_{i,t}$ is the price of security *i* in *t*

$D_{i,t}$ is the dividend including all other effects which have to be accounted for.

Continuous returns $r_{i,t}^{cont.}$ are given by

Formula 14:

$$r_{i,t}^{cont.} = log\left(\frac{P_{i,t} + D_{i,t}}{P_{i,t-1}}\right) = log\left(r_{i,t}^{discr.} + 1\right)$$

$$= log\left(P_{i,t} + D_{i,t}\right) - log\left(P_{i,t-1}\right)$$

A comprehensive discussion of the different characteristics of discrete and continuous returns can be found in Dorfleitner (2002). One main difference between both methods can be found when returns are cumulated over several periods.

Formula 15:

$$r_{i,T}^{discr.} = \prod_{t=1}^{T} (1 + r_{i,t}^{discr.}) - 1$$

where $r_{i,t}^{discr.}$ = constant for all t

Formula 16:

$$r_{i,T}^{cont.} = \sum_{t=1}^{T} r_{i,t}^{cont.}$$

where $r_{i,t}^{cont.}$ = constant for all t

While continuous returns can simply be added as *Formula 15* shows, the aggregation of discrete returns is more complicated (*Formula 16*).

Another advantage of continuous returns arises from the distribution from returns. As investors in stocks have limited liability, the price of a stock $P_{i,t}$ cannot be negative. *Formula 13* shows that then

$$r_{i,t}^{discr.} \geq -1$$

While this reflects on the one hand the economics of stock returns properly, on the other hand discrete returns cannot be assumed to be normally distributed. As normal distribution is an essential assumption of many statistical methods, continuous returns are more likely to satisfy this assumption (Röder, 1999: 14).

Nevertheless, discrete returns have advantages as well. As Barber and Lyon (1997) show, continuous returns underestimate returns structurally. But for small returns, the difference is not crucial. Dorfleitner (2002: 218) shows that continuous and discrete returns for small returns are approximately equal.

$$r_{i,t}^{discr.} \approx r_{i,t}^{cont.} \text{ for small } r_{i,t}$$

Because of the described advantages, in this study returns are calculated continuously.

When calculating returns, dividend payments have to be incorporated as *Formula 14* shows. Therefore, the Total Return Index (*RI*) of Datastream is used. The *RI* shows the overall growth of the value of a stock when dividends are reinvested.

IV.2.b.2 Modeling Normal Returns

To analyse the impact of an event on stock prices, the normal returns which would have been realized without the event have to be estimated in a first step. Literature provides several models to calculate normal returns. MacKinlay (1997:17) separates these models into statistical and economic models. While statistical models are solely based on statistical assumptions, economic models are mainly based on assumptions on investors' behaviour. Discussions on different models can, for instance, be found in Brown, Warner (1980) Strong (1992, 536 et seqq.), MacKinlay (1997: 17 et seqq.) or Röder (1999: 23 et seqq.). The most common models will be described in this chapter.

Constant Mean Return Model

The Constant Mean Return Model of Masulis (1980: 153 et seqq.) assumes that normal returns are constant in the estimation and the event period.

Brown and Warner find in their study that even though the Constant Mean Return Model does not adjust for any risk factors, the results are even better than those of complicated models under certain circumstances (1980: 249).

Formula 17: $r_{i,t} = \sum_{k=1}^{T} \frac{r_{i,k}}{T} + \varepsilon_{i,t}$ *with*

$$E(\varepsilon_{i,t}) = 0$$

$$cov(\varepsilon_{i,t}, \varepsilon_{i,s}) = 0$$

Market Model

Sharpe developed the Market Model in 1963, which has become the most common model for estimating normal returns (Strong, 1992: 537 and Röder, 1999: 23). The Market Model presumes that securities' returns are a linear function of market returns.

Formula 18: $r_{i,t} = \alpha + \beta_i \cdot r_{Market} + \varepsilon_{i,t}$

The study by Brown and Warner concludes that the market risk is the main risk factor (1980: 249). Armitage (1995: 31) finds that the market model is powerful when the shares have the same event date. During bull and bear markets, the results of the market model are biased. However, the market model is one of the most popular models in event studies (Strong, 1992: 537).

Capital Asset Pricing Model

Markowitz provides a groundbreaking normative model to explain optimal portfolio selection and investor behavior (1952). In a further development, Sharpe (1964) and Lintner (1965) derive the Capital Asset Pricing Model (CAPM). The CAPM explains risk premiums and security prices and provides a simple model to calculate them. Because of its simplicity and because the CAPM is one of few models that is based on an economic theory and is not solely driven statistically, the CAPM has become one of the most important models to calculate stock prices in science as well as in practice (Strong, 1992: 536).

The expected return of security i in t can be calculated by the risk free rate, the expected market return and the risk factor β_i.

Formula 19: $$E(r_{i,t}) = r_{f,t} + \beta_i \cdot (E(r_{Market}) - r_{f,t}) \text{ and}$$

Formula 20: $$r_{i,t} = r_{f,t} + \beta_i \cdot (r_{Market} - r_{f,t}) + \varepsilon_{i,t}$$

Formula 21: $$\beta_i = \frac{\sigma_{i,Market}}{\sigma^2_{Market}}$$

The CAPM states that risk premiums are only paid for the systematic risk of each security, which is defined by β_i. The idiosyncratic risk which can be diversified yields no risk premium.

Criticisms focus on the several assumptions of the CAPM that describe a neoclassical world (see Manner/Mankiw/Weil, 1997: 182 or Kruschwitz/Husmann 2012: 188 et seqq.). Since the CAPM was established, a significant number of papers have tried to prove if beta is dead or alive. Fama, French (1996b), Röder (1999: 25) and Wulff (2001: 125) provide an overview over these studies.

Three Factor Model by Fama/French

Fama and French extend the Capital Asset Pricing Model by adding two further risk factors (Fama/French, 1992: 433 et seqq.). These two risk factors cover most return anomalies of the CAPM (Fama/French 1996b: 1948). One big disadvantage of the Three Factor Model is the high data demand which arises from the three factor regression (Röder, 1999: 28)

Formula 22:

$$r_{i,t} = \alpha + \beta_{1,i} \cdot (r_{Market} - r_{f,t}) + \beta_{2,i} \cdot SMB_t + \beta_{3,i} \cdot HML_t + \varepsilon_{i,t}$$

SMB is the return difference of small firms and large firms.

HML is the return difference of firms with high book-to-market ratios and low book-to-market ratios.

A detailed description how *SMB* and *HML* have to be calculated can be found in Fama/French (1996a: 58).

Arbitrage Pricing Theory

Besides the CAPM, the Arbitrage Pricing Theory (APT) by Ross (1976) is another well-known economic model to calculate stock returns. In contrast to the CAPM, the APT is not based on a portfolio theory and investors behavior but on the assumption of arbitrage-free markets. Analogous to other models, returns are a linear function of risk factors. In a first step, the arbitrage portfolio is generated, which is completely diversified and therefore virtually riskless. In arbitrage-free markets, the return of security i can then be derived and takes the form

Formula 23: $$r_{i,t} = \alpha + \sum_{k=1}^{N} \beta_{k,i} \cdot F_{k,t} + \varepsilon_{i,t}$$

A detailed derivation can be found in Padberg (1995: 2012 et seqq.). If the APT is reduced to one risk factor for market risk, it equals the CAPM. Therefore, the CAPM can be considered as a special form of the APT. Brown/Weinstein (1985) try to validate the APT empirically and find that the explanatory power of the APT is not superior compared to the simple market model.

IV.2.c Statistical Estimation of Normal and Abnormal Returns

To estimate the β-coefficients, the estimation period has to be defined. This study uses the same estimation period and event window as the study by Gebhardt/Entrup/Heiden (1994).

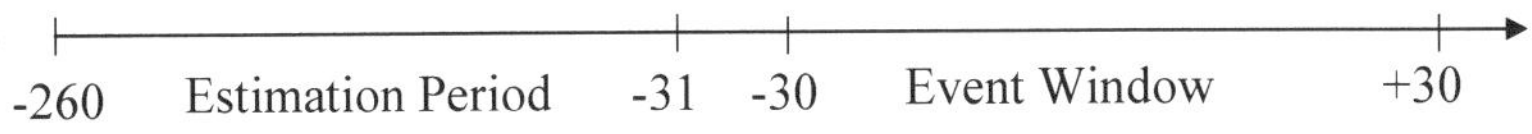

Figure 2: The Chronological Set-Up.

Within the period of [-260; +30], 34 firms of the sample were listed or delisted. This reduces the sample size to 164. The theoretical market model of the CAPM cannot be observed. Therefore, the logarithmic market returns are derived from the major German stock index, the DAX30. This index includes the 30 most important exchange listed companies of Germany. The risk-free rate is taken from the 1-year German Treasury Bill whose rates are provided by the International Monetary Fund. Using this data, the β-coefficient for each firm can be calculated in a simple linear regression using the ordinary least-squares estimation.

The abnormal returns are estimated by subtracting the expected returns from the observed returns.

Formula 24: $$AR_{i,t} = r_{i,t} - E(r_{i,t}) = \varepsilon_{i,t}$$

To cumulate the abnormal returns over a period $[T_s; T_e]$, the daily abnormal returns simply are added.

Formula 25: $$CAR_{i,T_s,T_e} = \sum_{t=T_s}^{T_e} AR_{i,t}$$

After calculating the abnormal returns and the cumulative abnormal returns, the mean cumulative abnormal returns $MCAR_{T_s;T_e}$ have to be estimated.

Therefore, the cumulative abnormal returns for each firm are added and then divided by the total number of firms *N* (Strong 1992: 540).

Formula 26: $$MCAR_{T_s,T_e} = \frac{1}{N}\sum_{i=i}^{N} CAR_{i,T_s,T_e}$$

IV.2.d Test of Significance

After calculating the *CAR*s, it is necessary to test whether the results are statistically significant. As *CAR*s of stock dividends are expected to be positive, the null hypothesis can be set up.

Formula 27: $$H_0: CAR \leq 0$$

$$H_1: CAR > 0$$

For the statistical analysis, this study uses parametric and non-parametric tests. A general overview over different tests can be found in Serra (2002). Armitage (1995: 47) provides an overview as to which test should be used in which scenario. MacKinlay (1995: 32) comes to the conclusion that studies typically rely on parametric tests and use non-parametric tests as a robustness check. This chapter highlights the main differences of the applied tests.

t-test

The most popular parametric test is the t-test. A description of the t-test can be found in Röder (1999: 46 et seqq.). The main assumptions are that the *AR*s and the *CAR*s are independent and normally distributed. Especially the second assumption that returns are normally distributed is satisfied better by using continuous returns. For this reason, returns are calculated continuously in this study (see *Chapter IV.2.b.1*). Still, several studies find that the distribution of returns has fat tails compared to a normal distribution and are right-skewed (see Brown/Warner, 1985: 4 or Serra, 2002: 7). However Brown/Warner further finds no impact of the non-normal distribution of returns on event studies (1985: 25). They further claim that at least the mean abnormal returns are distributed just about normally for larger sample sizes.

Corrado Rank Test

Armitage (1995: 42 et seq.) states that non-paramectric sign tests are often used in event studies, although they tend to reject the null hypothesis too rarely. The huge advantage of non-parametric tests is that they do have less assumptions compared to the t-test. Specifically, there is no assumption concerning the distribution of the returns. Therefore, non-parametric tests are superior for small sample sizes when returns are not normally distributed. The rank test of Corrado (1989) deals with the bias of the sign test. In a first step, the *AR*s of the estimation period and the event period are sorted from high to low. Then the ranks of the returns in the event period are compared with the rank of the returns in the estimation period. The Corrado test needs less assumptions than the non-parametric sign test and is resistant to an increase of the variance of *AR*s in the event window (see Corrado, 1989: 394 et seq.). Armitage (1995: 47) comes to the same conclusion, that the Corrado test can be used in most scenarios. Gebhardt/Entrup/Heiden (1994) rely on the Corrado test exclusively in their empirical analysis of German stock dividends. However, Corrado states that the advantages of the Corrado test decrease for longer periods (1989: 395). Nevertheless, the t-test is advantageous when used in ideal conditions.

Wilcoxon-Mann-Whitney Test

The Wilcoxon-Mann-Whitney test which is also known as the u-test was developed by Wilcoxon (1945) and Mann, Whitney (1947). This test analyzes whether two distributions are equal or not. This study uses the test to compare the *CAR*s of different subsamples. The hypothesis can be setup as follows:

Formula 28:

$$H_0\text{: } CAR_{Sample\ 1} = CAR_{Sample\ 2}$$

$$H_1\text{: } CAR_{Sample\ 1} \neq CAR_{Sample\ 2}$$

Feltovich (2002: 274 et seq.) gives a description of the computation of the Wilcoxon-Mann-Whitney test. First, the *CAR* of each firm in sample 1 is compared with the *CAR*s of each firm in sample 2. Each firm in sample 1 is placed on the basis of the number of firms with lower *CAR*s in sample 2. Then the mean placement is linked to a test statistic to provide levels of significance.

IV.3 Proxy for Jensen's Free Cash Flow

To analyze whether *CAR*s of firms with high *FCF* are lower (see *Chapter III.1.d*), the high free cash flow firms have to be identified first. The balance sheet provides information about the cash flow after all implemented projects have been funded. These projects might include projects with a negative net present value. Thus the *FCF* cannot be directly observed. Therefore, different studies (Lehn/Poulsen, 1989, Lang/ Stulz/Walkling, 1991, McCabe/Yook, 1997) use a proxy to estimate which firms have high *FCF* and which firms do not. The studies mentioned all use the same basic idea in how to create a proxy for *FCF*.

Firms with a high *FCF* must have a high cash flow on the balance sheet before investments. But not all firms with a high cash flow do necessarily have high *FCF*. Firms with high growth opportunities have a wide range of projects with positive net present value. In contrast, firms with high cash flow but little growth opportunities have only limited valuable projects. Hence, firms with a high cash flow before investment, which have little growth opportunities, are most likely to have a high *FCF*.

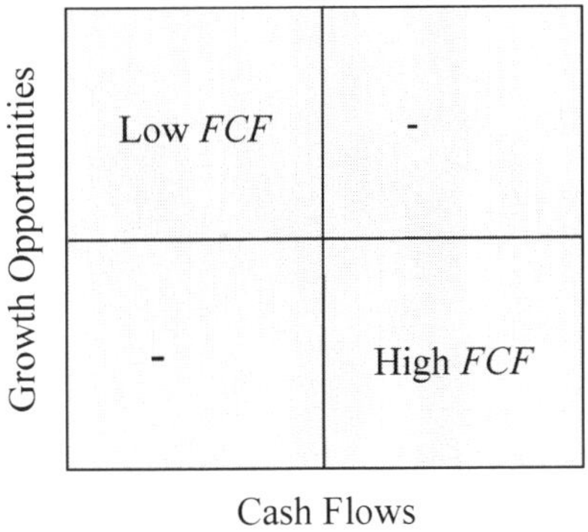

Figure 3: The Proxy for Free Cash Flow.

While the cash flow can be derived from the balance sheet, the growth opportunities of the firm are more difficult to measure. Lehn and Poulsen (1989) use sales growth over the last years. One considerable problem in using sales growth as a proxy for growth opportunities is that the sales growth might be the consequence of prior investment in a negative net present value project (Lehn/Poulsen, 1989: 777 et seq.). An empire building manager of a firm with high *FCF* might use the *FCF* to acquire another firm, even if this acquisition would have a negative net present value. Due to the acquisition the manager's firm would have a high sales growth not because of good growth opportunities but simply because of the prior empire building business policy of the management. Therefore, Lang/Stulz/Walkling (1991) and McCabe/Yook (1997) use Tobin's q to determine the growth opportunities of a firm to incorporate the market's assessment. Tobin's q is the ratio of the total market value of the firm divided by the replacement costs of the firm's assets.

Formula 29:

$$Tobins\ q = \frac{Market\ Value\ Equity + Market\ Value\ Debt}{Replacement\ Costs}$$

Firms with high growth opportunities should be assessed higher by the market participants and, hence, have a higher *Tobin's q* than firms with low growth opportunities.

A German characteristic is the prevalence of bank loans compared to bonds. Therefore, it is hard to estimate the market value of debt. This study uses the book value of debt instead of the market value. *Replacement Costs* are approximated by using the book value of the firm.

Formula 30:

$$q = \frac{Market\ Value\ Equity + Book\ Value\ Debt}{Total\ Book\ Value\ of\ the\ Firm}$$

The cash flow is calculated in this study by using the definition by Lang/Stulz/Walkling (1991: 319) and McCabe/Yook (1997: 706). As the cash flow has to be normalized in respect to the firm's size, Lang/Stulz/Walkling divide the cash flow by *Total Assets*.

Formula 31:

$$CF = \frac{1}{Total\ Assets} \cdot (Operating\ Income\ before\ Depreciation - Interest\ Expenses - Total\ Dividends - Tax)$$

q and *CF* are estimated for each firm by using the data from the annual statement of the year prior to the event employing data from Datastream. As the data required is not available for every firm, the number of events is reduced to 126. The firms are separated as shown in *Figure 3*. Therefore the sample is splitted at the median into, high-/low cash flow firms and firms with high-/low Tobin's q. This means that in our study firms with a *q* below the sample medians *q* and *CF* higher than the sample medians *CF* are assumed to have high *FCF*.

V Data Analysis

V.1 Announcement Effect of Stock Dividends

V.1.a Estimation of Abnormal Returns

Abnormal returns are calculated by using the capital asset pricing model. As the theoretical market portfolio cannot be observed, this study uses DAX returns. For the robustness test, the main findings will alternatively be tested with the market model and with MDAX returns.

The Durbin-Watson test indicates for all models that there is no first-stage serial correlation of the residuals. Since R^2 is low for all models, the explanatory power is weak. However, these results are comparable to other studies for the German market (see *Chapter III.2.b*). Furthermore, the t-test shows that all parameters are significantly positive.

	Parameters	Mean	Standard Deviation	t-Test	R^2	Adjusted R^2	Durbin-Watson
Dax	CAPM						
	β	0.44973	0.43524	14.31770***	0.06103	0.05672	1.83964
	Market Model						
	α	0.00191	0.00382	6.92832***	0.06959	0.06099	1.85643
	β	0.43923	0.42998	14.15444***			
MDAX	CAPM						
	β	0.74257	0.64662	15.91244***	0.05439	0.05005	1.84544
	Market Model						
	α	0.00203	0.00405	6.94473***	0.06394	0.05529	1.86374
	β	0.73514	0.64650	15.75629***			

*** Rejection of the null hypothesis: Parameter ≤ 0 with alpha < 0.5 percent

** Rejection of the null hypothesis: Parameter ≤ 0 with alpha < 1.0 percent

* Rejection of the null hypothesis: Parameter ≤ 0 with alpha < 5.0 percent

Table 9: Estimated Parameters for the Period [-260; -31].

V.1.b Analysis of Abnormal Returns

V.1.b.1 Cumulative Abnormal Returns for the Total Sample

Calculating mean cumulative abnormal returns for the whole sample of 192 events, a strong positive market reaction in the announcement period can be found.

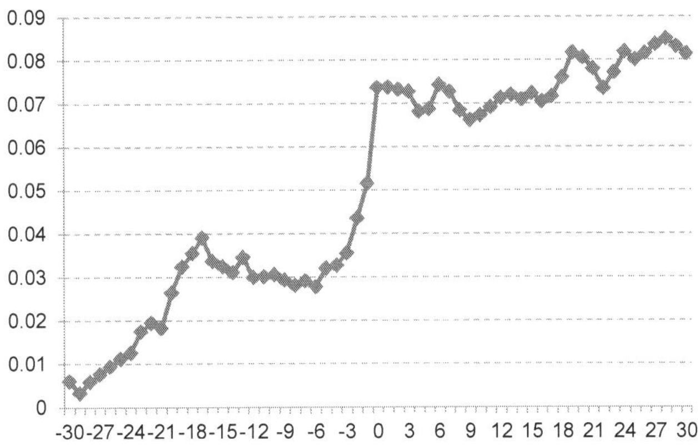

Figure 4: Mean Cumulative Abnormal Returns, Total Sample.

The absolute amount of *MCAR*s in the event window [-30; +30] is higher than in other studies. While Gebhardt/Entrup/Heiden (1994) find *MCAR*s of 6.46 percent, this study estimates *MCAR*s of 8.13 percent[17]. Equally, both studies find positive *MCAR*s 30 days prior to the event and a slight, insignificant decrease in *MCAR*s starting on the day after the event.

The positive *MCAR*s in the period [-30; -1] might be caused by insider trading. Besides, it can be argued that the announcement dates are estimated too late. As LexisNexis does not cover all news, information about the stock dividends might have reached the market earlier.

[17] As the sample of Gebhardt/Entrup/Heiden (1994) ends in 1990, the samples are not overlapping.

Period	MCAR	t-value	Corrado	Positive Sign
[0]	0.02213	4.34298***	5.39913***	64.63%
[-1; 0]	0.03019	5.26174***	5.63401***	67.68%
[-3; +1]	0.04111	5.65172***	5.43437***	63.41%
[-3; +3]	0.04018	5.27205***	4.77735***	65.24%
[-10; +10]	0.03722	3.55362***	2.44389**	62.80%
[-30; +30]	0.08131	4.06859***	2.35011**	64.02%
[-3; -1]	0.01890	3.5856***	3.46124***	56.71%
[-30; -1]	0.05147	3.29036***	0.81005	57.93%
[+1; +3]	-0.00085	-0.17269	0.7191	50.61%
[+1; +30]	0.00771	0.74342	1.55535	57.32%

n 164

*** Rejection of the null hypothesis: MCAR ≤ 0 with alpha < 0.5 percent

** Rejection of the null hypothesis: MCAR ≤ 0 with alpha < 1.0 percent

* Rejection of the null hypothesis: MCAR ≤ 0 with alpha < 5.0 percent

Table 10: MCARs and Test of Significance, Total Sample.

Table 10 shows that the *CAR*s are highly significant for all periods, except for the two periods tested after the announcement [1;3] and [1;30]. The significance for the longer periods using the Corrado test is slightly lower. Here, it has to be taken into account that the Corrado test is limited when it comes to testing longer periods (see *Chapter IV.2.d*).

V.1.b.2 Diluted Events

Unfortunately, announcements of stock dividends are often diluted. In this sample, only 64 of the 164 firms in the total sample announce stock dividends without releasing any other information. Regarding *Figure 5*, there the *MCAR*s almost match for the diluted and the undiluted events.

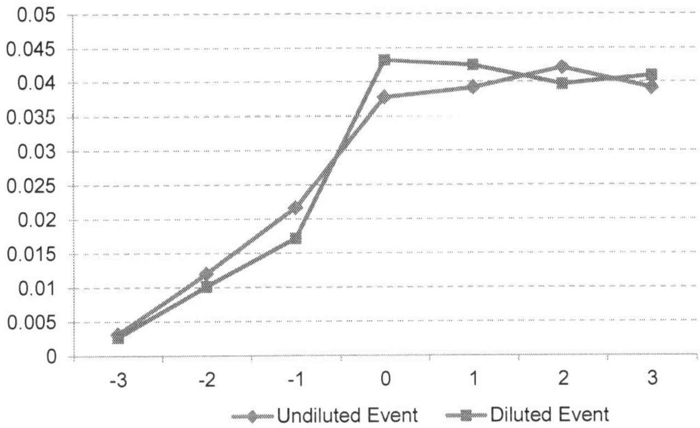

Figure 5: MCARs of Diluted and Undiluted Events.

To investigate if the difference between *CAR*s of the total sample and the undiluted announcements is significant, a dummy for the undiluted events can be incorporated in a linear regression model.

Formula 32: $$CAR = c + b * Dummy_{Undiluted\ Events}$$

The results for three different event windows [0], [-3; +1]; [-3; +3] and [-30; +30] show that the difference is not significant at all (see *Table 12*). As the dilution of the news contains additional positive information in some events and additional negative information in others, the effects of dilution seem to counterbalance. To keep the sample size as high as possible for further analysis, the diluted announcements are not deleted from the sample.

Period	MCAR	t-value	Corrado	Positive Sign
[0]	0.01607	3.87276***	3.31829***	64.06%
[-1; 0]	0.02570	4.7273***	3.42802***	67.19%
[-3; +1]	0.03909	3.36826***	3.21399***	65.63%
[-3; +3]	0.03911	3.18788***	2.26369*	67.19%
[-10; +10]	0.02852	1.75031*	-0.20912	59.38%
[-30; +30]	0.06869	2.31096*	-0.12467	64.06%
[-3; -1]	0.02163	2.05412*	1.95679*	57.81%
[-30; -1]	0.06278	2.39242**	0.21851	57.81%
[+1; +3]	0.00141	0.21094	-0.41476	51.56%
[+1; +30]	-0.01015	-0.63918	-1.00211	50.00%

n 64

*** Rejection of the null hypothesis: MCAR ≤ 0 with alpha < 0.5 percent

** Rejection of the null hypothesis: MCAR ≤ 0 with alpha < 1.0 percent

* Rejection of the null hypothesis: MCAR ≤ 0 with alpha < 5.0 percent

Table 11: MCARS and Test of Significance, Undiluted Announcements.

	Variable	Coefficient	Std. Error	t-Statistic	Prob.
	C	0.02601	0.00655	3.97223	0.00011
CAR_0	Dummy Undiluted Event	-0.00994	0.01048	-0.94819	0.34444
	C	0.04241	0.00937	4.52499	0.00001
$CAR_{-3;+1}$	Dummy Undiluted Event	-0.00332	0.01500	-0.22101	0.82536
	C	0.04087	0.00982	4.16179	0.00005
$CAR_{-3;+3}$	Dummy Undiluted Event	-0.00176	0.01572	-0.11209	0.91089
	C	0.08939	0.02573	3.47402	0.00066
$CAR_{-30;+30}$	Dummy Undiluted Event	-0.02070	0.04119	-0.50257	0.61595

Table 12: Linear Regression Model, CARs, Undiluted Announcements, Formula 32.

V.1.b.3 Special Distributions

Chapter V.1.b.2 analyzes whether diluted events influence the results of *MCAR*s. Within the subsample of diluted events there were 10 firms which announced special distributions together with the stock dividend. As distributions to shareholders affect stock prices, the firms with special distributions are investigated separately.

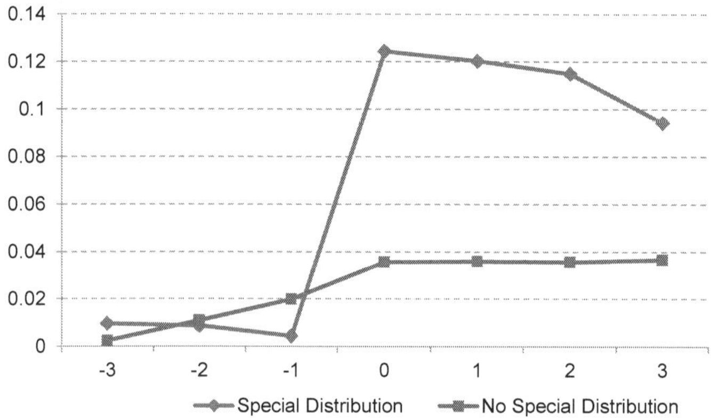

Figure 6: MCARs of Special Distributions.

Figure 6 displays very high *MCAR*s for the special distribution firms. However, the results are only significant at a low level (see *Table 13*). The main reason might be the small sample size of 10 firms.

To analyze whether the difference between the firms with and without special distributions is significant, a dummy for the firms with special distributions is incorporated into a linear regression model.

Formula 33: $$CAR = c + b * Dummy_{Special\ Distribution}$$

Period	MCAR	t-value	Corrado	Positive Sign
[0]	0.12004	2.09148*	1.95526*	70.00%
[-1; 0]	0.11569	1.92034*	1.05519	70.00%
[-3; +1]	0.12032	2.46265*	1.57045	80.00%
[-3; +3]	0.09430	2.25245*	0.08009	80.00%
[-10; +10]	0.09952	1.59917	0.48263	70.00%
[-30; +30]	0.19205	4.29613***	1.15642	90.00%
[-3; -1]	0.00435	0.33953	0.42358	70.00%
[-30; -1]	0.05148	2.5415*	0.89603	80.00%
[+1; +3]	-0.03008	-0.96343	-1.43011	50.00%
[+1; +30]	0.02053	0.67296	0.39599	70.00%

n	10
***	Rejection of the null hypothesis: MCAR ≤ 0 with alpha < 0.5 percent
**	Rejection of the null hypothesis: MCAR ≤ 0 with alpha < 1.0 percent
*	Rejection of the null hypothesis: MCAR ≤ 0 with alpha < 5.0 percent

Table 13: MCARs and Test of Significance, Special Distributions.

	Variable	Coefficient	Std. Error	t-Statistic	Prob.
CAR_0	C	0.01577	0.00489	3.22614	0.00152
	Dummy Spec. Distr.	0.10427	0.01980	5.26703	0.00000
$CAR_{-3;+1}$	C	0.03597	0.00737	4.87816	0.00000
	Dummy Spec. Distr.	0.08435	0.02986	2.82455	0.00533
$CAR_{-3;+3}$	C	0.03667	0.00783	4.68046	0.00001
	Dummy Spec. Distr.	0.05763	0.03173	1.81643	0.07115
$CAR_{-30;+30}$	C	0.07412	0.02062	3.59386	0.00043
	Dummy Spec. Distr.	0.11793	0.08352	1.41196	0.15988

Table 14: Linear Regression Model, CARs, Special Distributions, Formula 33.

Table 14 shows that the dummy is significant for the event windows [0] and [-3;1]. In order to take the small sample size into account, the non-parametric Wilcoxon-Mann-Whitney test is calculated in addition to the t-test. The Wilcoxon-Mann-Whitney test corroborates the significance for the periods [-3;1] and [-30;30] (see *Table 15*).

	Value	Prob.
CAR_0	1.54965	0.12122
$CAR_{-3;+1}$	2.03757	0.04159
$CAR_{-3;+3}$	1.82454	0.06807
$CAR_{-30;+30}$	2.19563	0.02812

Table 15: Wilcoxon-Mann-Whitney Test, MCARs and Special Distribution.

Period	MCAR	t-value	Corrado	Positive Sign
[0]	0.01577	4.70232***	5.07183***	64.29%
[-1; 0]	0.02463	5.6905***	5.53926***	67.53%
[-3; +1]	0.03597	5.23945***	5.20453***	62.34%
[-3; +3]	0.03667	4.84939***	4.9011***	64.29%
[-10; +10]	0.03318	3.21709***	2.39654**	62.34%
[-30; +30]	0.07412	3.53747***	2.13115*	62.34%
[-3; -1]	0.01985	3.58027***	3.45931***	55.84%
[-30; -1]	0.05147	3.09935***	0.60997	56.49%
[+1; +3]	0.00105	0.21923	1.09902	50.65%
[+1; +30]	0.00688	0.63323	1.50296	56.49%

n 154

*** Rejection of the null hypothesis: MCAR ≤ 0 with alpha < 0.5 percent

** Rejection of the null hypothesis: MCAR ≤ 0 with alpha < 1.0 percent

* Rejection of the null hypothesis: MCAR ≤ 0 with alpha < 5.0 percent

Table 16: MCARs and Test of Significance, No Special Distribution.

As the *MCAR*s for the firms with special distributions are very high, these firms might have a major impact on the total sample. From *Table 14* it follows that the fixed effect for the sample is positive on a highly significant level. Thus, the positive *MCAR*s of the total sample are not mainly driven by the special distribution forms. Analyzing the *MCARs* of the firms without special distributions separately confirms that the announcement effect remains positive on a high significance level (see *Table 16*)

V.1.b.4 Euro Converters

As discussed in *Chapter IV.1.c*, 21 firms in the sample announced stock dividends to correct odd nominal values which resulted from the introduction of the Euro in 1999. Since those firms only made an optical correction, the stock market effect to the announcement should be less pronounced than for other firms.

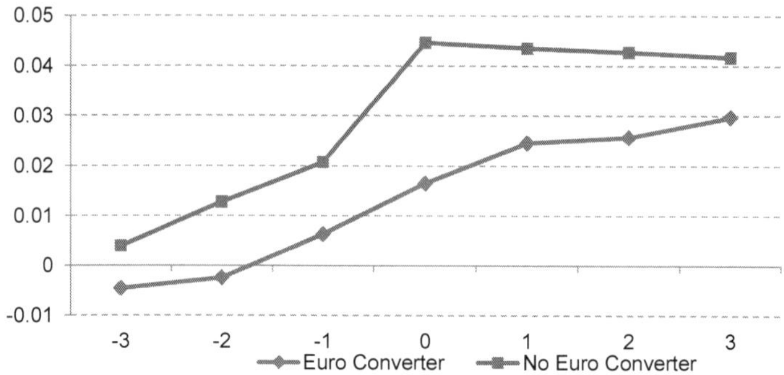

Figure 7: MCARs of Euro Converters.

Figure 7 shows that the *MCAR*s of the euro converters are lower than the *MCAR*s of the rest of the sample. *Table 17* shows that the *MCAR*s still are significantly positive at least on a 5 percent level.

Period	MCAR	t-value	Corrado	Positive Sign
[0]	0.01018	2.24276*	1.83604*	61.90%
[-1; 0]	0.01901	2.80521**	2.15398*	66.67%
[-3; +1]	0.02459	2.17187*	1.89929*	71.43%
[-3; +3]	0.02973	2.37481*	2.12858*	76.19%
[-10; +10]	0.02027	1.10166	1.97603*	57.14%
[-30; +30]	-0.01225	-0.31991	1.42235	47.62%
[-3; -1]	0.00636	0.67089	0.66844	47.62%
[-30; -1]	-0.00906	-0.43053	0.26189	38.10%
[+1; +3]	0.01318	1.44268	1.52298	52.38%
[+1; +30]	-0.01337	-0.39477	1.4311	38.10%

n	21
***	Rejection of the null hypothesis: MCAR ≤ 0 with alpha < 0.5 percent
**	Rejection of the null hypothesis: MCAR ≤ 0 with alpha < 1.0 percent
*	Rejection of the null hypothesis: MCAR ≤ 0 with alpha < 5.0 percent

Table 17: MCARs and Test of Significance, Euro Converters.

Testing the regression model *Formula 34* in *Table 18* shows that the dummy for the euro converters is negative but not significant for all the event windows tested.

Formula 34:

$$CAR = c + b * Dummy_{EuroConverters}$$

As discussed in *Chapter IV.1.d*, the split ratios of the euro converting firms are very high, which also suggests that the *MCAR*s should be lower. It thus can be argued that the euro conversion effect is also covered by the split ratio effects, which will be analyzed in the following chapter.

	Variable	Coefficient	Std. Error	t-Statistic	Prob.
	c	0.02388	0.00548	4.36083	0.00002
CAR_0	Dummy Euro Converters	-0.01370	0.01530	-0.89504	0.37209
	c	0.04354	0.00782	5.56764	0.00000
$CAR_{-3;+1}$	Dummy Euro Converters	-0.01895	0.02185	-0.86708	0.38718
	c	0.04172	0.00821	5.08414	0.00000
$CAR_{-3;+3}$	Dummy Euro Converters	-0.01199	0.02293	-0.52303	0.60167
	c	0.09505	0.02132	4.45792	0.00002
$CAR_{-30;+30}$	Dummy Euro Converters	-0.10730	0.05959	-1.80075	0.07360

Table 18: Linear Regression Model, CARs, Euro Converters, Formula 34.

V.1.b.5 Split Ratio Effects

The scale of both the retained earnings hypothesis and the liquidity hypothesis depends on the split ratio (see *Chapter III.2.b.2* and *Chapter III.2.b.3*). The lower the split ratio (the higher the proportion of new shares issued) is, the greater the stock price is reduced. Thus, the liquidity effects should then be stronger. The same holds for retained earnings. As the low split ratio leads to a high reduction of retained earnings, the costs of false signaling and thereby the positive effect on the firm's value should increase.

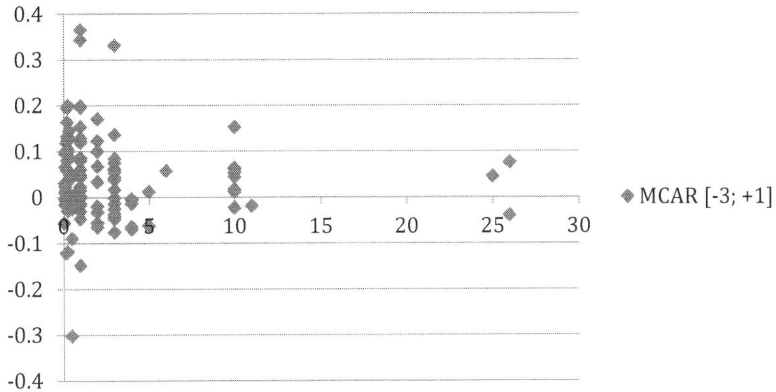

Figure 8: CARs in Dependence of Split Ratios.

Figure 8 plots the *CAR*s in dependence of the split ratios. In a first step, following Kaserer/Brunner (1997: 92), significance is tested by incorporating the split ratio into two different linear regression models.

Formula 35: $$CAR = c + b * Split\ Ratio$$

Formula 36: $$CAR = c + b * \frac{1}{Split\ Ratio}$$

Notwithstanding, in contrast to the results of Kaserer/Brunner (1997: 93), empirical evidence for the hypothesized negative correlation of split ratios and *MCAR*s cannot be found for any of the event windows tested (see *Table 19* and *Table 20*).

	Variable	Coefficient	Std. Error	t-Statistic	Prob.
CAR_0	c	0.01774	0.00454	3.90990	0.00015
	Split Ratio	-0.00106	0.00087	-1.20968	0.22878
$CAR_{-3;+1}$	c	0.04277	0.00952	4.49385	0.00002
	Split Ratio	-0.00109	0.00183	-0.59691	0.55169
$CAR_{-3;+3}$	C	0.04164	0.01029	4.04496	0.00009
	Split Ratio	-0.00098	0.00198	-0.49614	0.62070
$CAR_{-30;+30}$	c	0.09834	0.02868	3.42842	0.00083
	Split Ratio	-0.00622	0.00552	-1.12693	0.26202

Table 19: Linear Regression Model, CARs, Formula 35.

However, reconsidering *Figure 8*, *MCAR*s still seem to be a monotonically decreasing and convex function of the split ratio. As *MCAR*s should be close to zero for very high split ratios, it can be assumed that there are no fixed effects.

Formula 37: $lim(MCAR)_{Split\ Ratio \to \infty} = 0$

From this, the following linear regression model can be derived.

Formula 38: $CAR = b * \frac{1}{Split\ Ratio}$

	Variable	Coefficient	Std. Error	t-Statistic	Prob.
CAR_0	c	0.01872	0.00486	3.85220	0.00019
	1 / Split Ratio	-0.00151	0.00116	-1.30053	0.19591
$CAR_{-3;+1}$	c	0.04205	0.01022	4.11544	0.00007
	1 / Split Ratio	-0.00085	0.00244	-0.35018	0.72681
$CAR_{-3;+3}$	c	0.03758	0.01105	3.40125	0.00090
	1 / Split Ratio	0.00062	0.00263	0.23380	0.81550
$CAR_{-30;+30}$	c	0.08527	0.03092	2.75782	0.00670
	1 / Split Ratio	-0.00122	0.00737	-0.16574	0.86860

Table 20: Linear Regression Model, CARs, Formula 36.

	Variable	Coefficient	Std. Error	t-Statistic	Prob.
CAR_0	1 / Split Ratio	0.00112	0.00099	1.12931	0.26100
$CAR_{-3;+1}$	1 / Split Ratio	0.00504	0.00210	2.40486	0.01770
$CAR_{-3;+3}$	1 / Split Ratio	0.00588	0.00222	2.64797	0.00920
$CAR_{-30;+30}$	1 / Split Ratio	0.01073	0.00613	1.75239	0.08220

Table 21: Linear Regression Model, CARs, Formula 38.

Table 21 shows that the split ratio is highly significant for the event windows [-3; +1] and [-3; +3] if the linear regression model represented by *Formula 38* is used. These results provide further evidence for the retained earnings hypothesis and the trading range hypothesis and the positive effects of stock dividend announcements on stock prices.

But following Jensen's free cash flow hypothesis (see *Chapter III.1.d*), not only the positive but also the negative effects of stock dividends should be stronger for low split ratios. This might explain another major characteristic of the relationship of *CAR*s and split ratios (see *Figure 8*). For low split ratios, the variance of *CAR*s seems to be higher than for high split ratios. Regarding the linear regression model *Formula 38*, the squared residuals should thus be decreasing for higher split ratios.

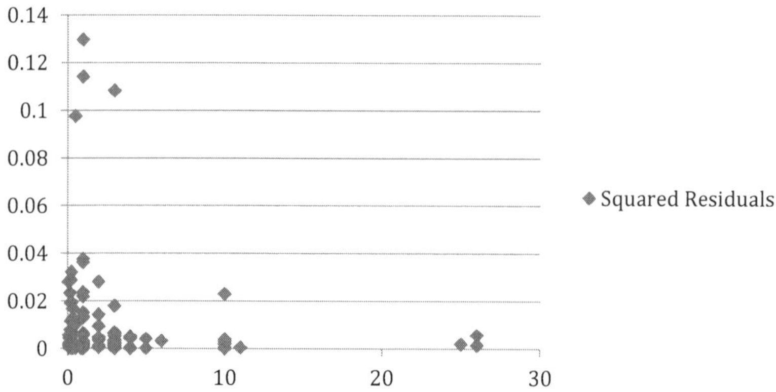

Figure 9: Squared Residuals in Dependence of Split Ratios, Formula 38, [-3; +1].

Regarding *Figure 9* the squared residuals seem to be a monotonically decreasing and convex function of the split ratio. Hence, a linear regression model should have the following form:

Formula 39: $$Resid^2 = b * \frac{1}{Split\ Ratio}$$

Table 22 shows that *Formula 39* is highly significant for the event windows [-3+1] and [+3:+3] and significant at least on a 4,133 percent level for [-30;+30]. Again, the event day itself [0] is not significant at all.

	Variable	Coefficient	Std. Error	t-Statistic	Prob.
$Resid^2_0$	1 / Split Ratio	0.00026	0.00022	1.21348	0.22731
$Resid^2_{-3;+1}$	1 / Split Ratio	0.00122	0.00048	2.53964	0.01236
$Resid^2_{-3;+3}$	1 / Split Ratio	0.00162	0.00050	3.25496	0.00147
$Resid^2_{-30;+30}$	1 / Split Ratio	0.00977	0.00474	2.06216	0.04133

Table 22: Linear Regression Model, Squared Residuals, Formula 39.

The influence of the split ratio on *CAR*s seems to be more complex than previous studies imply. First of all, this study can confirm the negative relationship of split ratios and *CAR*s. Beyond that, it can be shown that there seems to be negative effects of low split ratios for some firms, which cannot be equalized by the positive effects and lead to a high variance of *CAR*s for low split ratios.

V.1.b.6 Bonus Shares

Since 1998 there have been stock dividends without the issuance of bonus shares (see *Chapters II.1.b* and *II.1.c*). For these stock dividends, the number of shares does not change. If *MCAR*s continue to be positive for these firms, the theory that the positive effect of stock dividends is based solely on liquidity effects (see *Chapter III.1.c*) can be disproved.

In the total sample, only seven firms announced stock dividends without bonus shares. Unfortunately, the sample size is too small to get reliable results. However, analyzing these seven firms might give a first indication about the effects of stock dividends without bonus shares.

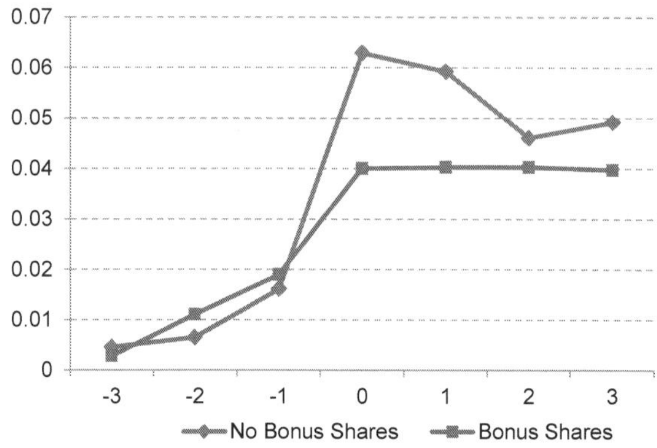

Figure 10: MCARs without Bonus Shares.

Figure 10 shows that *MCAR*s continue to be positive for firms in the sample, which do not issue bonus shares. Due to the small size of the subsample, the t-test and the Corrado test are not significant at all, although the *MCAR*s are positive for all the periods tested and the majority of *CAR*s has a positive sign (see *Table 23*).

Regarding *Figure 10*, the *MCAR*s of firms with and without bonus shares seem to be close together. The Wilcoxon-Mann-Whitney test confirms that there is no significant difference between the *MCAR*s of these two subsamples (see *Table 24*). Unfortunately, the sample size of stock dividends without bonus shares is too small for a profound analysis. Still, these results show that it is worth further investigation to provide a deeper understanding of liquidity effects of stock dividends.

Period	MCAR	t-value	Corrado	Positive Sign
[0]	0.04679	1.14853	1.44108	71.43%
[-1; 0]	0.05640	1.36563	1.78285	85.71%
[-3; +1]	0.05922	1.30906	1.57639	85.71%
[-3; +3]	0.04918	1.28054	1.33058	71.43%
[-10; +10]	0.05460	0.89534	0.63632	71.43%
[-30; +30]	0.08800	1.1067	0.67077	57.14%
[-3; -1]	0.01610	1.42203	1.41012	71.43%
[-30; -1]	0.00057	0.01149	-0.50727	42.86%
[+1; +3]	-0.01370	-0.90501	-0.20963	28.57%
[+1; +30]	0.04064	1.24034	1.20065	71.43%

n	7
***	Rejection of the null hypothesis: MCAR ≤ 0 with alpha < 0.5 percent
**	Rejection of the null hypothesis: MCAR ≤ 0 with alpha < 1.0 percent
*	Rejection of the null hypothesis: MCAR ≤ 0 with alpha < 5.0 percent

Table 23: MCARs and Test of Significance, No Bonus Shares.

	Value	Prob.
CAR_0	0.09762	0.92224
$CAR_{-3;+1}$	0.02440	0.98053
$CAR_{-3;+3}$	0.08948	0.92870
$CAR_{-30;+30}$	0.41488	0.67823

Table 24: Wilcoxon-Mann-Whitney Test, MCARs and Bonus Shares.

V.1.b.7 Cash Dividends

Following the retained earnings hypothesis, managers use stock dividends as a signal for further distributions to shareholders. Consequently, cash dividends should at least stay constant or even rise in the years after the stock dividend. Fama et al. (1969) find that stock dividends are frequently followed by increases of cash dividends. Gebhardt/Entrup/Heiden confirm this result for the German market (1994: 314). They find that 64 out of 69 firms increased cash dividends in the year of the announcement of the stock dividend. Even in the years after, cash dividends were only reduced in 9 cases.

This sample draws a less extreme but still similar picture of dividend policies following stock dividends. In the year of the announcement, 83 out of 109 increase their cash dividends. The percentage of firms that announce a reduction of cash dividends is quite low at 11.2 percent in the year of the announcement but rises up to 20.6 percent two years after the announcement.

The question arises whether investors can anticipate cash dividend growth as early as at the announcement day of the stock dividend. Therefore, cash dividend growth should be higher for firms with high *CAR*s. To focus on the anticipation effect, only firms without the explicit announcement of special distribution are taken into consideration.

Formula 40: $$Cash\ Dividend\ Growth = c + b * CAR$$

The growth rate of cash dividends is calculated for different periods. How cash dividends develop in reference to the cash dividends paid before the announcement of the stock dividend (Y_{-1}) has to be investigated first. Eight separate regressions with different event windows for the *CAR*s are calculated for each growth period and summarized in *Table 25*.

Table 25 provides several insights. First of all, most event periods cannot explain cash dividend growth from the years [-1; 0] and [-1; 1]. These findings are, so far, still in line with the retained earnings hypothesis. The fundamental idea of the retained earnings hypothesis is that managers expect high cash flows in the future. If cash flows were already high on the announcement day, there would be no information asymmetry with the investors and managers could simply increase the cash distributions.

Looking at future cash dividends, *Table 25* reveals that *CAR*s have a high explanatory power for cash dividend growth in the years [-1;2] and especially in [1;2].

However, it is surprising that on the day of the announcement [0], the *CAR*s are not significant for every dividend growth period regarded. This is especially unusual as the event period [0] shows the clearest and most significant effect in most other investigations of this study. A detailed inspection of the different event periods in *Table 25* shows that all four dividend growth rates tested can be explained by the *CAR*s of the period [-30;-1]. Thus, only inside traders who trade prior to the announcement can predict future cash dividend growth well. Investors who start trading at the announcement of the stock dividend or later cannot anticipate the future development of cash dividends.

		Variable	Coefficient	Std. Error	t-Statistic	Prob.
Cash Dividend Growth	Y_{-1} to Y_0	C	0.47817	0.11808	4.04940	0.00010
		CAR_0	-3.50610	3.30146	-1.06198	0.29094
		C	0.41646	0.11898	3.50037	0.00071
		$CAR_{-3;+1}$	0.20895	1.49395	0.13987	0.88906
		C	0.43524	0.11651	3.73564	0.00032
		$CAR_{-3;+3}$	-0.32471	1.30298	-0.24921	0.80374
		C	0.36997	0.10782	3.43145	0.00089
		$CAR_{-30;+30}$	0.96308	0.46383	2.07637	0.04056
		C	0.38858	0.11012	3.52855	0.00065
		$CAR_{-3;-1}$	2.12744	1.76311	1.20664	0.23057
		C	0.37851	0.10244	3.69506	0.00037
		$CAR_{-30;-1}$	1.85148	0.56832	3.25783	0.00156
		C	0.43462	0.10632	4.08767	0.00009
		$CAR_{+1;+3}$	-3.22021	2.40308	-1.34004	0.18343
		C	0.43092	0.10782	3.99665	0.00013
		$CAR_{+1;+30}$	-0.45259	0.90087	-0.50239	0.61655
	Y_{-1} to Y_{+1}	C	1.60560	0.68472	2.34491	0.02126
		CAR_0	-2.29775	18.86521	-0.12180	0.90333
		C	1.39081	0.69140	2.01157	0.04729
		$CAR_{-3;+1}$	5.15545	8.56455	0.60195	0.54874
		C	1.69953	0.67594	2.51434	0.01372
		$CAR_{-3;+3}$	-3.64915	7.43575	-0.49076	0.62481
		C	1.02917	0.59187	1.73885	0.08552
		$CAR_{-30;+30}$	9.78497	2.47554	3.95266	0.00015
		C	1.41358	0.64781	2.18207	0.03174
		$CAR_{-3;-1}$	8.67986	10.02964	0.86542	0.38913
		C	1.04196	0.51541	2.02162	0.04622
		$CAR_{-30;-1}$	18.52344	2.77008	6.68697	0.00000
		C	1.63078	0.60992	2.67376	0.00892
		$CAR_{+1;+3}$	-29.12784	13.83624	-2.10518	0.03809
		C	1.64773	0.62176	2.65011	0.00952
		$CAR_{+1;+30}$	-6.41622	5.10364	-1.25719	0.21198

Cash Dividend Growth	Y_{-1} to Y_{+2}	C	1.32866	0.61663	2.15471	0.03408
		CAR_0	25.92234	16.56406	1.56497	0.12139
		C	0.61502	0.57244	1.07438	0.28577
		$CAR_{-3;+1}$	29.94133	6.94128	4.31352	0.00004
		C	0.93885	0.59115	1.58818	0.11605
		$CAR_{-3;+3}$	20.26233	6.44804	3.14240	0.00232
		C	0.85021	0.49302	1.72448	0.08834
		$CAR_{-30;+30}$	12.51142	2.08538	5.99958	0.00000
		C	1.01732	0.52796	1.92689	0.05742
		$CAR_{-3;-1}$	36.82901	8.07731	4.55956	0.00002
		C	1.20195	0.46735	2.57181	0.01190
		$CAR_{-30;-1}$	15.71800	2.44623	6.42540	0.00000
		C	1.81935	0.55792	3.26093	0.00161
		$CAR_{+1;+3}$	-17.47156	12.59361	-1.38734	0.16905
		C	1.66943	0.56941	2.93184	0.00435
		$CAR_{+1;+30}$	3.98293	4.95744	0.80343	0.42402
	Y_{+1} to Y_{+2}	C	0.16968	0.10890	1.55803	0.12317
		CAR_0	5.43333	2.97246	1.82789	0.07129
		C	0.09711	0.10675	0.90967	0.36573
		$CAR_{-3;+1}$	4.17942	1.32304	3.15895	0.00223
		C	0.11083	0.10647	1.04100	0.30101
		$CAR_{-3;+3}$	3.60588	1.20741	2.98646	0.00374
		C	0.17663	0.10331	1.70968	0.09120
		$CAR_{-30;+30}$	0.97562	0.44011	2.21675	0.02948
		C	0.12370	0.09989	1.23841	0.21919
		$CAR_{-3;-1}$	6.30758	1.77872	3.54614	0.00066
		C	0.21421	0.09840	2.17701	0.03243
		$CAR_{-30;-1}$	1.13744	0.50881	2.23548	0.02817
		C	0.26061	0.09951	2.61904	0.01055
		$CAR_{+1;+3}$	-0.43670	2.22992	-0.19584	0.84524
		C	0.25872	0.10282	2.51632	0.01386
		$CAR_{+1;+30}$	0.01732	0.93561	0.01851	0.98528

Table 25: Cash Dividend Growth, Linear Regression Model

V.1.b.8 Market Value

Several studies affirm that Market Value (*MV*) influences abnormal returns in event studies. Following Merton's neglected firm hypothesis of 1987 (see *Chapter III.1.b.2.3*), small firms only try to attract investors' attention, for instance by stock dividends, when they believe that they are undervalued. Therefore, *MCAR*s should be lower for large firms. Regarding stock dividends in Germany, Gebhardt/Entrup/Heiden (1994: 323 et seqq.) form three groups of firms with high *MV*, average *MV* and low *MV*. They find that large firms have significantly lower *MCAR*s in the period of [-1,0].

This study confirms these results (see *Figure 11*, *Figure 12* and *Table 26*). However, in contrast to Gebhardt/Entrup/Heiden (1994), the results are significant for the long event window [-30;30]. The Wilcoxon-Mann-Whitney test validates the results of *Table 26* and finds a significant difference between the *MCAR*s of firms with high and low *MV* only for the period [-30;30] at a significance level of 2.8 percent.

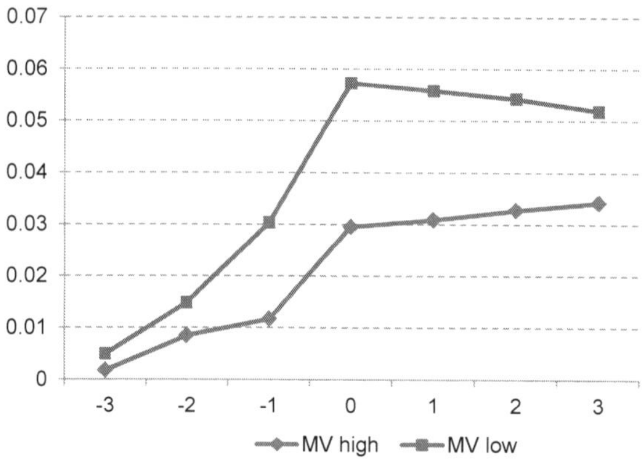

Figure 11: MCARs and Market Value [-3;3].

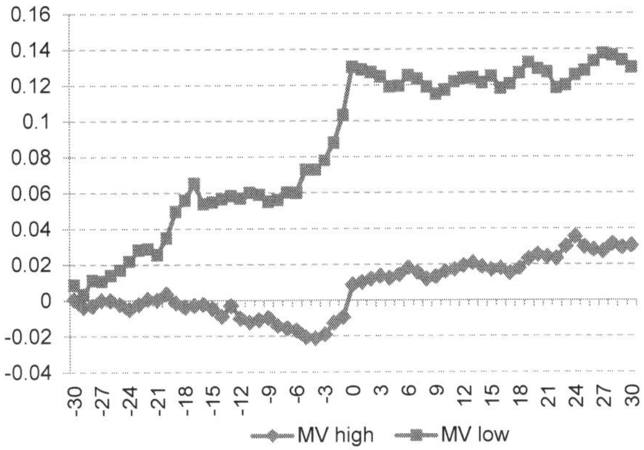

Figure 12: MCARs and Market Value [-30;30].

Formula 41: $CAR = c + b * Dummy_{MV\ low}$

In a next step, it will be analyzed whether there is a linear relationship between *CAR*s and *MV*. In summary, *Table 27* shows similar results. However, in contrast to the dummy regression, only the short event windows [-3;1] and [-3;3] are significant when *MV* is incorporated linearly into the regression model (see *Formula 42*). Nevertheless, this analysis delivers more support for the neglected firm hypothesis.

Formula 42: $CAR = c + b * MV$

	Variable	Coefficient	Std. Error	t-Statistic	Prob.
CAR_0	C	0.01798	0.00698	2.57521	0.01091
	Dummy MV low	0.00895	0.01026	0.87268	0.38413
$CAR_{-3;+1}$	C	0.02844	0.00988	2.87700	0.00456
	Dummy MV low	0.02736	0.01452	1.88398	0.06136
$CAR_{-3;+3}$	C	0.03010	0.01040	2.89268	0.00435
	Dummy MV low	0.02177	0.01528	1.42423	0.15630
$CAR_{-30;+30}$	C	0.03969	0.02703	1.46834	0.14395
	Dummy MV low	0.08983	0.03970	2.26250	0.02500

Table 26: Linear Regression Model, CARs, Market Value, Formula 41.

	Variable	Coefficient	Std. Error	t-Statistic	Prob.
CAR_0	C	0.02412	0.00567	4.25299	0.00004
	MV	-7.67523E-07	0.00000	-1.17346	0.24247
$CAR_{-3;+1}$	C	0.04764	0.00780	6.10883	0.00000
	MV	-1.91729E-06	0.00000	-2.13216	0.03462
$CAR_{-3;+3}$	C	0.04781	0.00793	6.02925	0.00000
	MV	-2.13418E-06	0.00000	-2.33408	0.02092
$CAR_{-30;+30}$	C	0.08597	0.02060	4.17300	0.00005
	MV	-2.73824E-06	0.00000	-1.15265	0.25089

Table 27: Linear Regression Model, CARs, Market Value, Formula 42.

V.2 Test of the Free Cash Flow Hypothesis

V.2.a Cash Flow and Tobin's q

In this chapter the hypothesis that firms with high *FCF* have lower cumulative abnormal returns in the event period than firms with low *FCF* is tested. Therefore, the proxy by Lang/Stulz/Walkling (1991) and McCabe/Yook (1997) is used which has been introduced in *Chapter IV.3*. To calculate *Cash Flow* (see *Formula 31* and Tobin's *q* (see *Formula 30*), data from Datastream is acquired. *Cash Flow* and Tobin's *q* are calculated with data from the last annual reports prior to the announcements.

In a first stage, the two variables *CF* and *q* are regarded separately. Therefore, high *CF* firms with low *CF* firms and high *q* firms with low *q* firms are compared.

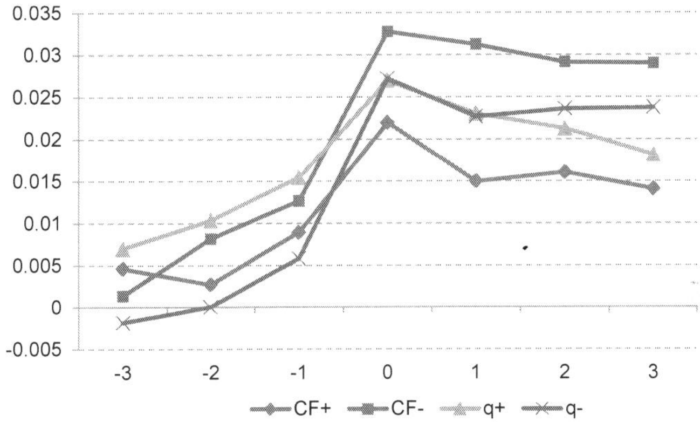

Figure 13: Subsamples CF and q: Mean Cumulative Abnormal Returns.

Period	MCAR	t-value	Corrado	Positive Sign
[0]	0.01397	3.54205***	3.90182***	67.24%
[-1; 0]	0.02207	3.88895***	3.87628***	68.97%
[-3; +1]	0.02076	1.8011*	1.89562*	58.62%
[-3; +3]	0.01884	1.54322	1.56908	56.90%
[-10; +10]	0.03599	2.40455**	1.50224	63.79%
[-30; +30]	0.06517	1.8844*	0.12891	62.07%
[-3; -1]	0.01296	1.52746	1.12118	53.45%
[-30; -1]	0.04645	1.67828*	-0.10095	56.90%
[+1; +3]	-0.00809	-1.24413	-0.97709	41.38%
[+1; +30]	0.00476	0.25295	-0.42759	60.34%

n	58
***	Rejection of the null hypothesis: MCAR ≤ 0 with alpha < 0.5 percent
**	Rejection of the null hypothesis: MCAR ≤ 0 with alpha < 1.0 percent
*	Rejection of the null hypothesis: MCAR ≤ 0 with alpha < 5.0 percent

Table 28: MCARs and Test of Significance, High Cash Flow.

Period	MCAR	t-value	Corrado	Positive Sign
[0]	0.03531	3.08456***	3.6797***	63.93%
[-1; 0]	0.03946	3.09937***	3.00877***	63.93%
[-3; +1]	0.04570	4.26224***	3.81951***	67.21%
[-3; +3]	0.04455	4.14295***	3.267***	70.49%
[-10; +10]	0.03802	2.48575**	1.76912*	63.93%
[-30; +30]	0.07865	3.15107***	2.36658*	67.21%
[-3; -1]	0.01487	2.57484**	2.54756**	54.10%
[-30; -1]	0.02192	1.36666	0.18543	55.74%
[+1; +3]	-0.00563	-0.70142	0.31839	49.18%
[+1; +30]	0.02142	1.642	2.51737**	59.02%

n	61
***	Rejection of the null hypothesis: MCAR ≤ 0 with alpha < 0.5 percent
**	Rejection of the null hypothesis: MCAR ≤ 0 with alpha < 1.0 percent
*	Rejection of the null hypothesis: MCAR ≤ 0 with alpha < 5.0 percent

Table 29: MCARs and Test of Significance, Low Cash Flow.

Period	MCAR	t-value	Corrado	Positive Sign
[0]	0.01096	3.20749***	2.74586***	63.16%
[-1; 0]	0.01946	4.15815***	3.66606***	71.93%
[-3; +1]	0.02608	3.11875***	2.92781***	59.65%
[-3; +3]	0.02638	2.61536**	2.90481***	57.89%
[-10; +10]	0.03131	2.64985**	2.97063***	63.16%
[-30; +30]	0.04164	1.48257	2.4989**	59.65%
[-3; -1]	0.01707	2.39971**	2.23535*	56.14%
[-30; -1]	0.02142	1.25019	0.78721	57.89%
[+1; +3]	-0.00165	-0.25354	0.61649	47.37%
[+1; +30]	0.00926	0.51877	2.27477*	59.65%

n	57
***	Rejection of the null hypothesis: MCAR ≤ 0 with alpha < 0.5 percent
**	Rejection of the null hypothesis: MCAR ≤ 0 with alpha < 1.0 percent
*	Rejection of the null hypothesis: MCAR ≤ 0 with alpha < 5.0 percent

Table 30: MCARs and Test of Significance, High Tobin's q.

Period	MCAR	t-value	Corrado	Positive Sign
[0]	0.02181	2.42473**	2.90823***	59.65%
[-1; 0]	0.02876	2.7677***	2.70497***	57.89%
[-3; +1]	0.03346	2.57707**	2.2788*	59.65%
[-3; +3]	0.03265	2.79399***	1.86135*	64.91%
[-10; +10]	0.04341	2.05114*	0.3498	63.16%
[-30; +30]	0.07245	2.05696*	-0.34647	63.16%
[-3; -1]	0.01268	1.54649	1.39642	57.89%
[-30; -1]	0.04988	1.78837*	-0.53274	54.39%
[+1; +3]	-0.00184	-0.21784	-0.23223	45.61%
[+1; +30]	0.00076	0.03987	-0.49227	54.39%

n	57
***	Rejection of the null hypothesis: MCAR ≤ 0 with alpha < 0.5 percent
**	Rejection of the null hypothesis: MCAR ≤ 0 with alpha < 1.0 percent
*	Rejection of the null hypothesis: MCAR ≤ 0 with alpha < 5.0 percent

Table 31: MCARs and Test of Significance, Low Tobin's q.

As *Figure 13*, *Table 28*, *Table 29*, *Table 30* and *Table 31* show, the *MCAR*s are positive for all four subsamples on a significant level. *Figure 13* also indicates that firms with high *CF* have lower *MCAR*s than firms with low *CF*.

As high *CF* is one of the two conditions for high *FCF*, this finding is in line with our hypothesis so far. Beyond that, a positive relationship between *MCAR*s and *CF* gives support for the retained earnings hypothesis. The retained earnings hypothesis postulates that managers would only transfer retained earnings into capital stock if they expect to generate enough *CF* in the future to keep the dividends at least constant. The risk not to be able to keep the dividends constant is higher for firms with low *CF*. Hence, managers of low *CF* firms have to be more convinced about extraordinary future business development than managers of high *CF* firms.

To test the relationship between *CAR*s and *CF*, a linear regression model is set up.

Formula 43: $$CAR = c + b * CF$$

Table 32 confirms the significant positive relationship between *CF* and *MCAR*s for the event periods [0]; [-3;+1] and [-3;+3]. These results provide further evidence for the retained earnings hypothesis.

Separating the firms into to subsamples with high *q* and low *q* (see *Figure 13*) shows no significant effects on *CAR*s at all.

	Variable	Coefficient	Std. Error	t-Statistic	Prob.
CAR_0	C	0.03081	0.00673	4.57642	0.00001
	CF	-0.11417	0.05177	-2.20527	0.02939
$CAR_{-3;+1}$	C	0.04191	0.00851	4.92391	0.00000
	CF	-0.16171	0.06545	-2.47069	0.01493
$CAR_{-3;+3}$	C	0.04009	0.00881	4.55081	0.00001
	CF	-0.15624	0.06775	-2.30601	0.02287
$CAR_{-30;+30}$	C	0.08676	0.02302	3.76928	0.00026
	CF	-0.28396	0.17701	-1.60420	0.11137

Table 32: Linear Regression Model, Cash Flow, Formula 43.

V.2.b Free Cash Flow Proxy

In a next step, both variables *CF* and *q* are combined to identify the firms with high *FCF*. Following *Figure 3*, those firms that have *CF (above median)* and at the same time a low Tobin's *q* (below median) are the high *FCF*-firms. As the main motivation for the managers of these firms, to execute stock dividends, might be binding capital to the company, the *MCAR*s of the high *FCF*-firms should be lower than for the rest of the sample.

Due to the high data demand to calculate *CF* and *q*, only 22 firms can be identified as *High FCF*-firms. This has to be taken into account when interpreting the t-values of the single groups (see *Table 33* and *Table 35*).

Figure 14 illustrates the *MCAR*s of the *High FCF* and the *No-FCF*-firms. In accordance with the hypothesis, the group of firms with *High FCF* has the lower *MCAR*s. *Table 33* shows the *MCAR*s for this subsample. The Corrado test is significant at a 5 percent level for the period [0]. The t-test finds positive *MCAR*s for the period [-1;0] at the same 5 percent level. In summary, there is nearly no announcement effect for *High FCF*-firms at all. The *No-FCF*-firms, however, have highly significant positive *MCAR*s as *Table 34* reveals.

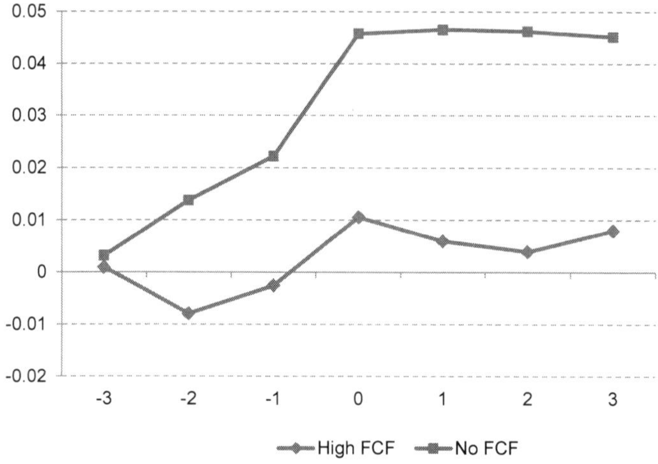

Figure 14: Mean Cumulative Abnormal Returns, FCF-Proxy.

Period	MCAR	t-value	Corrado	Positive Sign
[0]	0.01310	1.70799	2.0517*	59.09%
[-1; 0]	0.01847	1.85764*	1.57089	63.64%
[-3; +1]	0.00594	0.30898	0.81547	59.09%
[-3; +3]	0.00798	0.41828	0.70424	68.18%
[-10; +10]	0.02619	1.1208	-0.20069	59.09%
[-30; +30]	0.01458	0.38937	-2.47163	50.00%
[-3; -1]	-0.00255	-0.23415	0.02758	50.00%
[-30; -1]	-0.00528	-0.18947	-2.72194	36.36%
[+1; +3]	-0.00256	-0.22785	-0.13638	45.45%
[+1; +30]	0.00676	0.2307	-1.17707	63.64%

n	22
***	Rejection of the null hypothesis: MCAR ≤ 0 with alpha < 0.5 percent
**	Rejection of the null hypothesis: MCAR ≤ 0 with alpha < 1.0 percent
*	Rejection of the null hypothesis: MCAR ≤ 0 with alpha < 5.0 percent

Table 33: MCARs and Test of Significance, High FCF.

Period	MCAR	t-value	Corrado	Positive Sign
[0]	0.02353	4.08857***	5.04829***	65.49%
[-1; 0]	0.03200	4.97629***	5.46647***	68.31%
[-3; +1]	0.04656	6.00321***	5.51651***	64.08%
[-3; +3]	0.04517	5.50041***	4.85396***	64.79%
[-10; +10]	0.03893	3.37472***	2.67846***	63.38%
[-30; +30]	0.09165	4.12562***	3.36938***	66.20%
[-3; -1]	0.02223	3.83217***	3.68486***	57.75%
[-30; -1]	0.06026	3.45781***	1.81274*	61.27%
[+1; +3]	-0.00058	-0.10795	0.81506	51.41%
[+1; +30]	0.00786	0.70884	2.07015*	56.34%

n 142

*** Rejection of the null hypothesis: MCAR ≤ 0 with alpha < 0.5 percent

** Rejection of the null hypothesis: MCAR ≤ 0 with alpha < 1.0 percent

* Rejection of the null hypothesis: MCAR ≤ 0 with alpha < 5.0 percent

Table 34: MCARs and Test of Significance, No-FCF.

To test if *High FCF* can explain significantly the differences in *MCAR*s, a dummy for the *High FCF*-firms is incorporated into a linear regression model.

Formula 44: $$CAR = c + b * Dummy_{High\ FCF}$$

Table 35 only partially reveals evidence for the significance of the dummy *High FCF*. The period [-3;1] is significant on a 3.8 percent level, the period [-3;3] on a 5.4 percent level. The Wilcoxon-Mann-Whitney test (see *Table 36*) is not significant for any of the periods tested.

	Variable	Coefficient	Std. Error	t-Statistic	Prob.
	C	0.02394	0.00550	4.35668	0.00002
$MCAR_0$	Dummy High FCF	-0.01353	0.01500	-0.90139	0.36872
	C	0.04708	0.00776	6.06533	0.00000
$MCAR_{-3;+1}$	Dummy High FCF	-0.04444	0.02119	-2.09696	0.03755
	C	0.04597	0.00815	5.64277	0.00000
$MCAR_{-3;+3}$	Dummy High FCF	-0.04317	0.02225	-1.94049	0.05406
	C	0.09392	0.02144	4.38073	0.00002
$MCAR_{-30;+30}$	Dummy High FCF	-0.09401	0.05854	-1.60590	0.11024

Table 35: Linear Regression Model, Free Cash Flow, Formula 44.

	Value	Prob.
$MCAR_0$	0.55246	0.58064
$MCAR_{-3;+1}$	1.62360	0.10446
$MCAR_{-3;+3}$	1.43060	0.15255
$MCAR_{-30;+30}$	1.20865	0.22680

Table 36: Wilcoxon-Mann-Whitney Test, MCARs and High FCF.

It can be argued that firms with high *FCF* are on average more mature and thus larger. To control for size effects, *Formula 44* can be extended to

Formula 45:

$$CAR = c + b_1 * Dummy_{High\ FCF} + b_2 * Market\ Value$$

Table 37 shows that for all event windows tested, the significance of the *FCF* dummy increases.

As shown in *Chapter V.1.b*, a further relevant risk factor for modeling *CAR*s is the dummy variable for special distributions. For robustness tests, this variable is also incorporated into the regression model.

Formula 46:

$$CAR = c + b_1 * Dummy_{High\ FCF} + b_2 * Market\ Value$$

$$+ b_3 * Dummy_{Special\ Distribution}$$

For the event window [-3;1], all four variables of the regression are significant. Regarding the event window [-3;3], the fixed effect, the dummy for *High FCF* and the *Market Value* remain significant.

Previous studies focus on the positive effects of stock dividends. This study provides evidence that stock dividends are also used to detract capital from the investor. Still, the negative effects are balanced by the positive effects stock dividends have on stock prices. Therefore, even the subsample with *High FCF*-firms does not have negative *MCAR*s. However, the results are partially significant but not robust in other tests or certain event periods. Further work has to be done with other data sets for a thorough understanding of *FCF* and stock dividends.

	Variable	Coefficient	Std. Error	t-Statistic	Prob.
CAR_0	C	0.02651	0.00615	4.30883	0.00003
	Dummy High FCF	-0.01566	0.01563	-1.00182	0.31805
	Market Value	0.00000	0.00000	-1.25336	0.21204
$CAR_{-3;+1}$	C	0.05554	0.00832	6.67394	0.00000
	Dummy High FCF	-0.05178	0.02114	-2.44982	0.01545
	Market Value	0.00000	0.00000	-2.36523	0.01931
$CAR_{-3;+3}$	C	0.05569	0.00847	6.57623	0.00000
	Dummy High FCF	-0.05165	0.02151	-2.40120	0.01757
	Market Value	0.00000	0.00000	-2.56389	0.01134
$CAR_{-30;+30}$	C	0.10117	0.02219	4.55885	0.00001
	Dummy High FCF	-0.09961	0.05637	-1.76713	0.07925
	Market Value	0.00000	0.00000	-1.30488	0.19394

Table 37: Linear Regression Model, Free Cash Flow Formula 45.

	Variable	Coefficient	Std. Error	t-Statistic	Prob.
CAR_0	C	0.01806	0.00598	3.02139	0.00297
	Dummy High FCF	-0.00733	0.01464	-0.50086	0.61721
	Market Value	0.00000	0.00000	-0.95082	0.34324
	Dummy Spec. Distr.	0.10200	0.02075	4.91523	0.00000
$CAR_{-3;+1}$	C	0.04968	0.00856	5.80610	0.00000
	Dummy High FCF	-0.04601	0.02096	-2.19574	0.02967
	Market Value	0.00000	0.00000	-2.20443	0.02904
	Dummy Spec. Distr.	0.07070	0.02971	2.38008	0.01858
$CAR_{-3;+3}$	C	0.05219	0.00882	5.92050	0.00000
	Dummy High FCF	-0.04821	0.02159	-2.23277	0.02707
	Market Value	0.00000	0.00000	-2.45347	0.01531
	Dummy Spec. Distr.	0.04218	0.03061	1.37824	0.17021
$CAR_{-30;+30}$	C	0.09295	0.02313	4.01830	0.00009
	Dummy High FCF	-0.09151	0.05665	-1.61541	0.10835
	Market Value	0.00000	0.00000	-1.20447	0.23033
	Dummy Spec. Distr.	0.09920	0.08031	1.23525	0.21870

Table 38: Linear Regression Model, Free Cash Flow, Formula 46.

VI Conclusions

This study provides a comprehensive investigation of stock dividends. The analysis of the legal framework of the US reveals that the application of the retained earnings hypothesis on the US market is severely limited as distributable funds are in most cases not reduced by all types of stock distributions in the US. Furthermore, the accounting method which is essential for the retained earnings hypothesis is frequently not clear at the announcement date of stock distributions in the US.

In contrast, stock dividends in Germany lead to a direct reduction of distributable funds and the accounting method is always already determined in the announcement. Therefore, the German market is highly suitable to investigate the effects of the accounting method for stock dividends. Beyond that, it still has to be analyzed whether the change of accounting standards in Germany to international standards affects the retained earnings hypothesis.

Based on the analysis of the legal framework, the empirical findings of this study provide further evidence for the retained earnings hypothesis. The German stock corporation act permits stock dividends without issuing bonus shares. These transactions allow for an analysis of stock dividends excluding all liquidity effects. For these special transactions, *MCAR*s remain positive. Unfortunately, the size of this subsample in this study is too small for robust findings.

Further support for the retained earnings hypothesis results from the finding that the extent of *CAR*s is significantly positive correlated with future dividend growth. This means that investors can anticipate future dividend payments already in the event period. However, an in–depth investigation remarkably reveals that only inside investors that trade in the period prior to the announcement can estimate future dividend growth accurately. This should draw the attention of the financial supervisory agencies.

At the same time, this study reveals the limitations of the retained earnings hypothesis. For firms with a high *FCF*, the overinvestment hypothesis by Jensen seems to prevail. These firms seem to have lower *CAR*s than firms with low or average *FCF*s. Nevertheless, these results are not significant for all event windows tested. One reason might be the scope of the data set. Given larger data sets, it might be especially promising to analyse stock dividends without bonus share. Initial evidence from this study, that the announcement effects remain significant even without the issuance of bonus shares, could then be investigated more thoroughly.

Stock distributions are often considered to be thoroughly investigated and understood. In point of fact, interesting research questions still arise from stock distributions.

Appendices

Appendix 1: Distribution of Stock Splits and Stock Dividends of German Stocks Listed in the Official Market of the FSE (Wulff, 1999: 21)

Year	Stock Splits		Stock Dividends	
	No.	Percent	No.	Percent
1960	1	0.4	34	3.0
1961	0	0.0	21	7.9
1962	0	0.0	10	3.7
1963	1	0.4	7	2.6
1964	0	0.0	4	1.5
1965	2	0.7	20	7.4
1966	6	2.2	15	5.6
1967	11	4.2	16	6.2
1968	11	4.4	8	3.2
1969	94	37.3	13	5.2
1970	14	5.6	9	3.6
1971	7	2.9	11	4.6
1972	6	2.6	6	2.6
1973	6	2.6	12	5.2
1974	7	3.0	11	4.7
1975	0	0.0	7	3.1
1976	4	1.8	10	4.5
1977	2	0.9	8	3.7
1978	2	0.9	3	1.4

1979	2	0.9	6	2.8
1980	1	0.5	7	3.2
1981	3	1.4	11	5.0
1982	2	0.9	7	3.2
1983	1	0.5	9	4.1
1984	3	1.3	9	3.9
1985	0	0.0	4	1.7
1986	0	0.0	8	3.1
1987	1	0.4	10	3.8
1988	3	1.1	9	3.3
1989	0	0.0	12	4.1
1990	2	0.6	14	4.5
1991	2	0.6	7	2.2
1992	1	0.3	11	3.4
1993	1	0.3	10	3.0
1994	4	1.2	8	2.3
1995	38	10.8	11	3.1
1996	38	10.7	9	2.5
Total	276		387	

Appendix 2: Firms in the Sample

AACH.UND MUNCH.VERS.REGD

ABACHO

ACHTERBAHN

ADCAPITAL

ADIDAS

AIXTRON

ALBIS LEASING

ALLBECON

ALLGEIER HOLDING

ALLIANZ LEBENS-VICHERUNG

ALTANA (XET)

ANDREAE-NORIS ZAHN

ARQUES INDUSTRIES

B I S BOERSEN INFO.

BAADER WERTPAH.

BAYERISCHE IMMO-BILIEN

BEIERSDORF

BERLINER EFFEKTEN

BEWAG 'A'

BID BOERSENINFOR-MATION

BIJOU BRIGITTE

BIODATA INFO.TECH.

BMP

BMW

BOSS (HUGO)

BUSINESS MEDIA CHINA

BWIN (FRA)

CDV SOFTWARE ENTM.

CE GLOBAL SOURCING

CENIT SYSTEMHAUS

COMMERZBANK

COMPUTER 2000

CONCORD EFFEKTEN

CONERGY

CTS EVENTIM

DAIMLERCHRYSLER

DATA MODUL

DATADESIGN

DEUTSCHE BOERSE

DKM WERTPAH.

DOCCHECK

DT.HYPBK.FRANKFURT

DT.STEINZEUG CMBRG

ELRINGKLINGER

EM TV

ERGO VERSICHERUNG

ERLUS

ESCOM

EVOTEC

FIAT

FPB HOLDING

FREENET

FRESENIUS

FROSTA

FUCHS PETROLUB

GAUSS INTERPRISE

GEHE

GENERALI

GFK

GFN

GFT TECHNOLOGIES

GILDE BRAUEREI

GILDEMEISTER

GOLD-ZACK

GTG DIENSTLEISTUNGS

HANSA GROUP

HEIDELBERGCEMENT

HEILIT + WOERNER BAU

HERMLE BERTHOLD PF.

HEYDE

HOCHTIEF

HUETTENWERK KAYSER

IFA SYSTEMS

IMPERA

INTICOM SYSTEMS

IPC ARCHTEC

IVG IMMOBILIEN
KAMPA
KAMPS
KENVELO
KINOWELT MEDIEN
KLING JELKO DEHMEL
KLOECKNER-WERKE
KOENIG & BAUER
KOLB & SCHUELE
KST BETEILIGUNGS
KWS SAAT
LINTEC INFO.TECH.
LINZ TEXTIL
LOBSTER NET.STORAGE
LOEWENBRAEU
LPKF LASER & ELTN.
MARKT &KUEHLHALLEN
MAX AUTOMATION
MDB
MEDION
METRO
MICROLOGICA
MLP
MOBILCOM
MWB WERTPAPIERHANDELS
NOVASOFT
NUERNBERGER BET.
NUERNBERGHYP
OMV
ONVISTA
PAUL HARTMANN
PEGASUS BET.PREF.
PLENUM
PLETTAC
PONAXIS
PONGS & ZAHN
PORSCHE PREF.
QIAGEN
RHOEN-KLINIKUM
RSE GRUNDBESITZ UND BET.

RTV FAMILY ENTM.

SAP

SCHERING

SENATOR ENTERTAINMENT

SER SYSTEME

SIEMENS

SINGULUS TECHNOLOGIES

SINNERSCHRADER

SINO

SOFTLINE

SOFTM SFTW.BERATUNG

SOLARWORLD

SPRINGER (AXEL)

STADA ARZNEIMITTEL

STO PREF.

STOLBERGER TELECOM

STRABAG

STRATEC BIOMEDICAL SYS.

STUTT.HOFBRAEU

SUEDZUCKER

SYSKOPLAN

SYZYGY

TDS INFORMATIONS TECH.

TECIS HOLDING

TELES

THIEL LOGISTIC

THURINGIA VERS.

TRIA IT-SOLUTIONS

UNITED INTERNET

UNYLON

USU SOFTWARE

VBH HOLDING

VCL FILM + MEDIEN

VERBUND AKT

VIVACON

VOLKSFUERSORGE HDG

VOSSLOH

WCM BETEILIGUNG

WEBER (GERRY) INTL.

WUERTT.HYPOBANK

ZEAG ENERGIE

Appendix 3: Size of the Firms in the Year prior to the Announcement

Cross-section	TotalAssets	Total Sales	Market Value
Datastream Item	*392*	*104*	*MV*
CS001			53,380,000
CS003	3,846,548,000	4,711,621,000	2,071,750,000
CS004	71,809,000	95,454,000	99,400,000
CS005	1,471,448,000	1,689,626,000	531,290,000
CS006			149,120,000
CS007			14,028,520,000
CS008	381,164,000	1,820,412,000	149,090,000
CS009	301,481,000	497,299,000	442,500,000
CS010	54,344,000	58,489,000	71,040,000
CS011	24,445,000	1,632,000	23,890,000
CS012	552,236,000	424,975,000	1,092,120,000
CS013	92,591,000	150,918,000	154,920,000
CS014	120,874,000	256,883,000	101,360,000
CS015	182,596,000	343,296,000	118,700,000
CS016	45,145,296,000	7,689,041,000	3,435,880,000
CS017	138,609,000	133,532,000	118,240,000

CS018	158,434,000	273,464,000	60,130,000
CS020	174,478,000	196,098,000	317,510,000
CS021	2,208,298,000	1,609,891,000	2,454,200,000
CS022	315,338,000	51,355,000	
CS023	8,449,393,000	2,296,717,000	709,160,000
CS025	26,809,000	4,314,000	129,740,000
CS026	106,382,000	292,732,000	60,590,000
CS028	1,679,520,000	2,634,484,000	2,179,640,000
CS029	52,979,000	62,750,000	55,590,000
CS030	556,690,000	71,440,000	1,038,940,000
CS031	11,456,000	36,617,000	16,310,000
CS033	112,466,000	202,219,000	
CS036	112,466,000	202,219,000	
CS037	111,988,000	112,739,000	83,520,000
CS038	11,851,284,000	804,877,000	232,350,000
CS040	1,479,203,000	946,059,000	519,780,000
CS041	29,654,000	14,765,000	25,060,000
CS043	148,709,000	279,997,000	235,190,000
CS044	4,646,145,000	3,087,457,000	1,771,630,000
CS045	9,612,287,000		
CS047	58,534,448,000	10,358,448,000	3,321,350,000

CS048	248,789,000	394,870,000	202,470,000
CS049	1,601,872,000	952,873,000	489,900,000
CS050	18,281,344,000	1,058,155,000	361,230,000
CS051	23,310,000	24,332,000	
CS052	18,942,000	253,000	138,950,000
CS053	39,324,000	135,680,000	
CS054	790,098,000	832,429,000	107,410,000
CS056	72,227,000	78,949,000	36,240,000
CS057	4,994,069,000	2,171,806,000	1,752,460,000
CS058	70,114,000	121,997,000	
CS059	1,747,091,000	1,032,878,000	977,370,000
CS060	297,142,000	580,964,000	370,030,000
CS061	39,883,000	209,000	29,350,000
CS062	916,767,000	449,758,000	561,400,000
CS063	67,955,648,000	11,664,277,000	5,588,670,000
CS064	7,749,000	7,946,000	
CS066	319,190,000	230,210,000	793,010,000
CS067	51,943,000	39,775,000	274,820,000
CS068	633,000	2,160,000	
CS069	27,646,560,000	30,747,552,000	12,659,640,000
CS070	21,207,424,000	1,236,852,000	395,740,000

CS071	3,574,000	6,802,000	
CS072	259,856,928,000	17,053,104,000	16,796,540,000
CS073	61,478,912,000	14,847,512,000	3,038,760,000
CS074	56,765,000	82,811,000	226,710,000
CS075	297,142,000	580,964,000	370,030,000
CS076	2,195,620,000	3,424,774,000	5,486,060,000
CS078	42,709,000	54,896,000	
CS079	25,587,000	28,002,000	105,380,000
CS080	5,510,324,000	3,145,351,000	2,541,120,000
CS081	726,168,000	399,956,000	730,690,000
CS082	39,883,000	209,000	29,350,000
CS083	25,689,000	23,632,000	26,830,000
CS084	1,482,528,000	1,249,997,000	83,860,000
CS085			55,220,000
CS087	18,038,000	36,981,000	
CS088	32,590,000	85,067,000	
CS089	23,023,000	12,994,000	185,600,000
CS090	152,617,000	155,131,000	73,380,000
CS091	300,587,000	444,543,000	107,570,000
CS092	19,013,000	15,699,000	26,080,000
CS093	17,466,000	31,493,000	

CS094	866,111,000	747,742,000	74,610,000
CS095	6,197,000	13,784,000	
CS096	72,599,000	65,953,000	651,170,000
CS097	41,935,000	65,580,000	
CS098	59,951,000	2,607,000	63,500,000
CS099	161,111,000	131,197,000	73,710,000
CS100	416,554,000	449,976,000	78,910,000
CS101	69,083,000	60,848,000	
CS102	3,607,601,000	3,884,555,000	1,770,510,000
CS103	15,144,000	4,060,000	4,350,000
CS104	38,417,000	9,157,000	252,550,000
CS105	63,552,000	322,749,000	
CS106			82,010,000
CS107	4,618,000	2,931,000	
CS108	443,673,000	304,716,000	1,616,400,000
CS109	16,710,000	7,197,000	53,170,000
CS110	13,899,303,000	3,115,380,000	289,290,000
CS111	1,567,599,000	2,621,811,000	405,720,000
CS112	104,514,000	169,312,000	276,100,000
CS113	135,162,992,000	131,782,000,000	84,253,190,000
CS114	78,503,472,000	13,656,573,000	4,595,490,000

CS115	3,172,973,000	4,328,236,000	22,144,040,000
CS116	23,080,000	27,785,000	
CS117	4,567,351,000	3,285,086,000	7,311,760,000
CS118	57,823,000	55,172,000	783,550,000
CS119	30,148,000	18,915,000	61,350,000
CS121	85,254,000	183,660,000	39,450,000
CS122	61,743,000	95,865,000	575,200,000
CS123	1,926,000	674,000	
CS124	11,129,000	20,343,000	
CS125	27,691,000	31,616,000	119,640,000
CS126	33,140,000	18,164,000	
CS127	13,722,000	15,047,000	
CS128	2,255,000	4,489,000	
CS129	17,942,000	988,000	
CS130	46,004,000	70,489,000	119,850,000
CS131	44,605,000	4,610,256,000	106,700,000
CS132	1,525,836,000	2,459,892,000	2,433,750,000
CS133	22,275,000	16,327,000	150,320,000
CS134	12,111,000	20,311,000	
CS135	12,859,000	25,983,000	
CS136	91,070,000	99,064,000	885,930,000

CS137	14,339,000	11,996,000	
CS138	37,643,000	22,315,000	
CS139	274,373,000	254,355,000	132,530,000
CS140	29,926,000	31,377,000	81,480,000
CS141	2,905,000	321,230	5,370,000
CS143	470,466,000	754,286,000	584,590,000
CS145	2,762,000	5,131,000	
CS146	26,605,000	7,308,000	
CS147	67,047,584,000	60,177,008,000	32,188,260,000
CS148	1,617,349,000	2,519,459,000	1,700,050,000
CS149	48,035,056,000	2,692,133,000	2,564,280,000
CS150	8,032,000	8,244,000	
CS151	135,661,000	84,655,000	2,163,000,000
CS152	5,503,000,000	4,952,000,000	636,400,000
CS153	68,881,000	115,666,000	
CS155	273,014,000	818,164,000	2,196,000,000
CS156	1,629,856,000	1,586,458,000	2,593,500,000
CS157	369,475,000	752,901,000	412,390,000
CS158	3,192,000	6,658,000	
CS159	2,445,947,000	335,069,000	7,051,130,000
CS160	60,439,000	37,719,000	109,200,000

CS161	1,251,362,000	195,018,000	1,143,430,000
CS163	33,786,000	45,434,000	11,450,000
CS164	11,717,500,000	6,688,800,000	2,938,470,000
CS165	65,218,000	17,627,000	43,800,000
CS166	674,542,000	940,006,000	79,650,000
CS167	72,400,000	30,899,000	52,000,000
CS168	912,915,000	557,742,000	36,720,000
CS169	51,088,000	95,305,000	81,810,000
CS171	48,010,000	53,972,000	71,860,000
CS172	61,919,000	85,625,000	19,960,000
CS173	53,337,000	15,660,000	29,430,000
CS174	28,605,000	28,717,000	19,730,000
CS175	36,395,000	13,278,000	29,520,000
CS176	320,156,000	392,521,000	144,240,000
CS177	464,457,000	559,373,000	326,520,000
CS178	731,427,000	633,548,000	713,380,000
CS179	90,053,000	42,224,000	83,440,000
CS180	86,412,000	19,542,000	91,220,000
CS182	17,492,000	2,343,000	3,620,000
CS183	7,504,515,000	7,644,432,000	3,188,160,000
CS184	1,101,800,000	956,300,000	765,500,000

CS185	28,088,000	39,054,000	7,500,000
CS186	8,512,000	6,364,000	10,490,000
CS187	5,936,884,000	4,841,932,000	3,955,000,000
CS188			160,750,000
CS189	142,656,000	224,382,000	124,200,000
CS191	6,146,285,000	7,024,606,000	42,142,030,000
CS192	427,297,000	424,276,000	372,900,000
CS193	17,673,000	824,000	5,160,000
CS194	3,840,000	5,311,000	
CS196			2,461,630,000
CS197	28,382,000	74,909,000	56,900,000
CS198	16,521,000	2,575,000	24,100,000
CS199	75,429,000	284,833,000	
CS200	46,586,000	6,947,000	42,540,000
CS202	272,600,000	199,900,000	402,520,000
CS203			1,630,000
CS204	25,635,000	40,442,000	55,600,000
CS205	137,058,000	55,537,000	119,360,000
CS206	140,069,000	128,570,000	117,950,000
CS207	252,294,000	509,683,000	1,162,120,000
CS208	55,737,000	15,651,000	50,520,000

CS209	21,166,000	3,004,000	3,910,000
CS210	2,677,000,000	4,546,000,000	7,224,000,000
CS211	16,125,000	19,457,000	25,930,000
CS212	75,692,000	123,509,000	18,170,000
Number of Data Points	180	179	151
Mean	5,812,836,922	2,348,779,376	2,255,516,424
Median	91,830,500	123,509,000	154,920,000

References

Armitage, Seth (1995):

EVENT STUDY METHODS AND EVIDENCE ON THEIR PERFORMANCE, in: "Journal of Economic Survey", Vol. 8, 1995, Issue 4, 25-52.

Avner, Arbel; ***Svanson***, Gene (1993):

THE ROLE OF INFORMATION IN STOCK SPLIT ANNOUNCEMENTS, in: "Quarterly Journal of Business and Economics", Vol. 32, 1993, Issue 2, 14-25.

Asquith, Paul; ***Healy***, Paul; ***Palepu***, Krishna (1989):

EARNINGS AND STOCK SPLITS, in: "The Accounting Review", Vol. 64, 1989, Issue 3, 387-403.

Barber, Brad. M.; **Lyon**, John. D. (1997):

DETECTING LONG-RUN ABNORMAL STOCK RETURNS: THE EMPIRICAL POWER AND SPECIFICATON OF TEST STATISTICS, in: "Journal of Financial Economics", Vol. 43, 1997, 341-372.

Bechmann, Ken L.; ***Raaballe***, Johannes (2007):

THE DIFERENCE BETWEEN STOCK SPLITS AND STOCK DIVIDENDS: EVIDENCE ON THE RETAINED EARNINGS HYPOTHESES, in: "Journal of Business Finance & Accounting, Vol. 34, 2007, Issues 3 & 4, 574-603.

Bhattacharya, Sudipto (1979):

IMPERFECT INFORMATION, DIVIDEND POLICY, AND "THE BIRD IN THE HAND" FALLACY, in: "Bell Journal of Economics", Vol. 10, 1979, Issue 1, 259-270.

Bhattacharya, Utpal; ***Daouk***, Hazem (2002):

THE WORLD PRICE OF INSIDER TRAIDING, in: "The Journal of Finance", Vol. 52, 2002, Issue 1, 75-108.

Binder, John H. (1998):

T*HE EVENT STUDY METHODOLOGY SINCE 1969*, in: "Review of Quantitative Finance and Accounting, Vol. 11, 1998, 111-137.

Brennan, Michael J.; ***Copeland***, Thomas E. (1988):

STOCK SPLITS, STOCK PRICES, AND TRANSACTION COSTS, in: "Journal of Financial Economics", Vol. 22, 1988, Issue 1, 83-101.

Brennan, Michael J.; ***Huges***, Patricia, J. (1991):

STOCK PRICES AND THE SUPPLY OF INFORMATION, in: "The Journal of Finance", Vol. 66, 1991, Issue 5, 1665-1691.

Brown, Stephen J., ***Warner***, Jerold B. (1980):

MEASURING STOCK PRICE PERFORMANCE, in: "Journal of Financial Economics", Vol. 8, 1980, 205-258.

Brown, Stephen J.; ***Weinstein***, Mark I. (1985):

DERIVED FACTORS IN EVENT STUDIES, in: "Journal of Financial Economics", Vol. 14, 1985, 491-495.

Burghof, Hans-Peter (1998):

DIE ÖKONOMISCHE FUNKTION VON NENNWERTAKTIEN, in: "Die Betriebswirtschaft", Vol. 58, 1998, Issue 4, 501-515.

Bhushan, Ravi (1989):

FIRM CHARACTERISTICS AND ANALYST FOLLOWING, in: "Journal of Accounting and Economics", Vol. 11, 1989, 255-274.

Canner, Niko; ***Mankiw***, N. Gregory; ***Weil***, David N. (1997):

AN ASSET ALLOCATION PUZZLE, in: "American Economic Review", Vol. 87, 1997, 181-191.

Copeland, T. E. (1979):

LIQUIDITY CHANGES FOLLOWING STOCK SPLITS, in: "Journal of Finance", Vol. 34, 1979, Issue 1, 115-141.

Corrado, Charles. J. (1989):

A NONPARAMETRIC TEST FOR ABNORMAL SECURITY-PRICE PERFORMANCE IN EVENT STUDIES, in: "Journal of Financial Economics", Vol. 23, 1989, 385-395.

Dolley, James D. (1933a):

CHARACTERISTICS AND PROCEDURE OF COMMON-STOCK SPLIT-UPS, in: "Harvard Business Review", Vol. 11, 1933, 316-326.

Dolley, James D. (1933b):

CHARACTERISTICS AND PROCEDURE OF COMMON-STOCK SPLIT-UPS – MOTIVES AND EFFECTS, in: "Harvard Business Review", Vol. 12, 1933, 70-81.

Crawford, D.; ***Franz***, D. R.; ***Lobo***, G. J. (2005):

SIGNALING MANAGERIAL OPTIMISM TROUGH STOCK DIVIDENDS AND STOCK SPLITS: A REEXAMINATION OF THE RETAINED EARNINGS HYPOTHESIS, in: "Journal of Financial and Quantitative Analysis", Vol. 40, 2005, Issue 3, 531-561.

Dorfleitner, Gregor (2002):

STETIGE VERSUS DISKRETE RENDITEN: ÜBERLEGUNGEN ZUR RICHTIGEN VERWENDUNG BEIDER BEGRIFFE IN THEORIE UND PRAXIS, in: "Kredit und Kapital", Vol. 35, 2002, Issue 2, 216-241.

Desai, Hemang; ***Jain***, Prem C. (1997):

LONG-RUN COMMON STOCK RETURNS FOLLOWING STOCK SPLITS AND REVERSE SPLITS, in: "Journal of Business", Vol. 70, 1997, Issue 3, 409-433.

Fama, Eugne F. (1970):

EFFICIENT CAPITAL MARKETS: A REVIEW OF THEORY AND EMPIRICAL WORK, in: "The Journal of Finance", Vol. 25, 1970, Issue 2, 383-417.

Fama, Eugene F. (1991):

EFFICIENT CAPITAL MARKETS: II, in: "The Journal of Finance", Vol.66, 1991, Issue 5, 1575-1617.

Fama, E. F.; ***Fisher***, L.; ***Jensen***, M. C.; ***Roll***, R. (1969):

THE ADJUSTMENT OF STOCK PRICES TO NEW INFORMATION, in: "International Economic Review", Vol. 10, 1969, Issue 1, 1-21.

Fama, E. F.; ***French***, K. (1992):

THE CROSS SECTION OF EXPECTED CROSS RETURNS, in: "The Journal of Finance", Vol 47, 1992, Issue 2, 427-465.

Fama, E. F.; ***French***, K. (1993):

COMMON RISK FACTORS IN RETURNS ON STOCKS AND BONDS, in: "Journal of Financial Economics", Vol. 33, 1993, Issue 1, 3-56.

Fama, E. F.; ***French***, K. (1996a):

MULTIFACTOR EXPLANATIONS OF ASSET PRICING ANOMALIES, in: "The Journal of Finance", Vol. 51, 1996, Issue 1, 55-84.

Fama, E. F.; ***French***, K. (1996b):

THE CAPM IS WANTED; DEAD OR ALIVE, in: "The Journal of Finance", Vol. 51, 1996, Issue 5, 1947-1958.

Feltovich, Nick (2003):

NONPARAMETRIC TESTS OF DIFFERENCES OF MEDIANS: COMPARISON OF THE WILCOXON-MANN-WHITNEY AND ROBUST RANK-ORDER TESTS, in: "Experimental Economics", Vol. 6, 2003, Issue 3, 273-297.

Foster III, T. W.; ***Scribner***, E. A. (1998):

ACCOUNTING FOR STOCK DIVIDENDS ANS STOCK SPLITS: CORRECTIONS TO TEXTBOOK COVERAGE, in: "Issues in Accounting Education", Vol. 13, 1998, Issue 1, 1-13.

Gebhardt, G.; ***Entrup***, U.; ***Heiden***, S. (1994):

KURSREAKTIONEN AUF KAPITALERHÖHUNGEN AUS GESELLSCHAFTSMITTELN, in: "Zeitschrift für Bankrecht und Bankwirtschaft", Vol. 6, 1994, Issue 4, 308-332.

Grinblatt, M. S.; ***Masulis***, R. W.; ***Titman***, S. (1984):

THE VALUATION EFFECTS OF STOCK SPLITS AND STOCK DIVIDEND, in: "Journal of Financial Economics", Vol. 13, 1984, Issue 4, 461-490.

Han, Ki C. (1995):

THE EFFECT OF REVERSE SPLITS ON THE LIQUIDITY OF THE STOCK, in: "Journal of Financial and Quantitative Analysis", Vol. 30, 1995, Issue 1, 159-169.

Harrison, D. A. (2000):

ZUR VORTEILHAFTIGKEIT VON AKTIENSPLITS, in: "Beiträge zum Rechnungs-, Finanz- und Revisionswesen", Vol. 48, 2000.

Heiden, S. (2002):

KURSREAKTIONEN AUF DIVIDENDENANKÜNDIGUNGEN, 2000, Gabler Edition Wissenschaft, 2002, Wiesbaden.

Heinkel, R. (1984):

A THEORY OF CREDIBILITY: COSTLESS SIGNALS IN A RATIONAL EXPECTATIONS; INFITITE HORIZON MODEL, in: "Working Paper", 1984, University of British Columbia, Vancouver.

Heinkel, R. (1982):

A THEORY OF CAPITAL STRUCTURE RELEVANCE UNDER IMPERFECT INFORMATION, in: "Journal of Finance", Vol. 37, 1982, Issue 5, 1141-1150.

Jensen, Michael C. (1986):

AGENCY COSTS OF FREE CASH FLOW, CORPORATE FINANCE, AND TAKEOVERS, in: "American Economic Review", Vol. 76, 1986, Issue 2, 323-329.

Jensen, Michael C. (1978):

SOME ANOMALOUS EVIDENCE REGARDING MARKET EFFICENCY, in: "Journal of Financial Economics", Vol. 6, 1978, 95-101

Jiraporn, Pornsit; ***Gleason***, Kimberly C. (2007):

DELAWARE INCORPORATION AND EARNINGS MANAGEMENT: AN EMPIRICAL ANALYSIS, in: "Journal of Applied Finance", Vol. 17, 2007, 40-51.

Kaserer, C.; ***Brunner,*** A. (1997):

DIE KURZ- UND LANGFRISTIGEN KURSEFFEKTE VON KAPITALERHÖHUNGEN AUS GESELLSCHAFTSMITTELN, in: "Finanzmarkt und Portfolio Management", Vol. 11, 1997, Issue 1, 77-99.

Krutschwitz, Lutz; ***Husmann***, Sven (2012):

Finanzierung und Investition, 7. Auflage, Oldenbourg Verlag, 2012, München.

Lakonishok, J.; ***Lev***, B. (1987):

STOCK SPLITS AND STOCK DIVIDENDS: WHY, WHO, AND WHEN, in: "Journal of Finance", Vol. 42, 1987, Issue 4, 913-932.

Lamoureux, Christopher G.; ***Poon***, Percy (1987):

THE MARKET REACTION TO STOCK SPLITS, in: "The Journal of Finance", Vol. 62, 1987, Issue 5, 1347-1370.

Lang, L. H. P.; ***Stulz***, R. M.; ***Walkling***, R. A. (1991):

A TEST OF THE FREE CASH FLOW HYPOTHESIS: THE CASE OF BIDDER RETURNS, in: "Journal of Financial Economics", Vol. 29, 1991, Issue 2, 315-336.

Lehn, K.; ***Poulsen***, A. (1989):

FREE CASH FLOW AND STOCKHOLDER GAINS IN GOING PRIVATE TRANSACTIONS, in: "Journal of Finance" Vol. 44, 1989, Issue 3, 771-787.

Leland, H. E.; ***Pyle***, D. H. (1977):

INFORMATIONAL ASYMMETRIES, FINANCIAL STRUCTURE, AND FINANCIAL INTERMEDIATION, in: "Journal of Finance", Vol. 32, 1977, Issue 2, 371-387.

Leuz, Christian; ***Deller***, Dominic; ***Stubenrath***, Michael (1998):

AN INTERNATIONAL COMPARISON OF ACCOUNTING-BASED PAYOUT RESTRICTIONS IN THE UNITED STATES, UNITED KINGDOM AND GERMANY, in: "Accounting and Business Research", Vol. 28, 1998, Issue 2, 111-129.

Lintner, John (1965):

THE VALUATION OF RISK ASSETS AND THE SELECTION OF RISKY INVESTMENTS IN STOCK PORTFOLIS AND CAPITAL BUDGETS, in: "The Review of Economics and Statistics", Vol. 47, 1965, 768-783.

MacKinlay, Craig A. (1997):

EVENT STUDIES IN ECONOMICS AND FINANCE, in: "Journal of Economic Literature", Vol. 35, 1997, 13-39.

Maloney, Michael T.; ***Mulherin***, J. Harold (1992):

THE EFFECTS OF SPLITTING ON THE EX: A MICROSTRUCTURE RECONCILIATION, in: "Financial Management", Vol. 21, 1992, 44-59.

Masulis, Ronald W. (1980):

THE EFFECTS OF CAPITAL STRUCTURE CHANGE ON SECURITY PRICES, in: Journal of Financial Economics, Vol. 8, 1980, 139-178.

Mann, H.B., ***Whitney*** D.R. (1947):

ON A TEST OF WHETHER ONE OF TWO RANDOM VARIABLES IS STOCHASTICALLY LARGER THAN THE OTHER, in: "The Annals of Mathematical Statistics", Vol. 18, 1947, 50-60.

Markowitz, Harry (1952):

PORTFOLIO SELECTION, in: "The Journal of Finance", Vol. 7, 1952, Issue 1, 77-91.

May, A. (1991):

ZUM STAND DER EMPIRISCHEN FORSCHUNG ÜBER INFORMATIONSVERARBEITUNG AM AKTIENMARKT: EIN ÜBERBLICK, in: "Zeitschrift für betriebswirtschaftliche Forschung", Vol. 43, 1991, Issue 4, 313-335.

McCabe, G. M.; ***Yook***, K. C. (1997):

JENSEN, MYERS-MAJLUF, FREE CASH FLOW AND THE RETURNS TO BIDDERS, in: "Quarterly Review of Economics & Finance", Vol. 37, 1997, Issue 3, 697-707.

McDaniel, Morey W. (1986):

BONDHOLDERS AND STOCKHOLDERS, in: "The Journal of Corporation Law", Vol. 13, 206-315.

McGough, Philip (1988):

THE LEGAL SIGNIFICANCE OF THE PAR VALUE OF COMMON STOCK: WHAT ACCOUNTING EDUCATORS SHOULD KNOW, in: "Issues in Accounting Education", Vol. 3, 1988, Issue 2, 330-350.

McNichols, Maureen; ***Dravid***, Ajay (1990):

STOCK DIVIDENDS, STOCK SPLITS, AND SIGNALING, in: "Journal of Finance", Vol. 45, 1990, Issue 3, 857-879.

Merton, Robert C (1987):

A SIMPLE MODEL OF CAPITAL MARKET EQUILIBRIUM WITH INCOMPLETE INFORMATION, in: "Journal of Finance", Vol. 42, 1987, Issue 3, 483-510.

Modigliani, Franco; ***Miller***, Merton H. (1958):

THE COST OF CAPITAL, CORPORATION FINANCE AND THE THEORY OF INVESTMENT, in: "American Economic Review", Vol. 48, 1958, Issue 3, 261-297.

Mohanty, Sunil; ***Moon***, Doocheol (2007):

DISENTANGLING THE SIGNALLING AND LIQUIDITY EFFECTS OF STOCK SPLITS, in: "Applied Financial Economics", Vol. 17, 2007, Issue 12, 979-987.

Murray, Dennis (1985):

FURTHER EVIDENCE ON THE LIQUIDITY EFFECTS OF STOCK SPLITS AND STOCK DIVIDENDS, in: "Journal of Financial Research", Vol. 8, Issue 1, 59-67.

Muscarella, Chris J.; ***Vetsuypens***, Michael R. (1996):

STOCK SPLITS: SIGNALING OR LIQUIDITY? THE CASE OF ADR 'SOLO- SPLITS', in: "Journal of Financial Economics", Vol. 42, , 1996, Issue 1, 3-26.

Myers, John H.; ***Bakay***, Archie J. (1948):

INFLUENCE OF STOCK SPLIT-UPS ON MARKET PRICE, in: "Harvard Business Review", Vol. 26, 1948, Issue 2, 251-265.

Padberg, Max (1995):

DER EINFLUSS VON KAPITALERHÖHUNGEN AUF DEN MARKTWERT DEUTSCHER AKTIENGESELLSCHAFTEN, in: "Finanzierung, Steuern, Wirtschaftsprüfung", Vol. 28, 1995.

Penman, Stephen H. (1983):

THE PREDICTIVE CONTENT OF EARNINGS FORECASTS AND DIVIDENDS, in: "Journal of Finance", Vol. 38, Issue 4, 1181-1199.

Peterson, Craig A.; ***Millar***, James A.; ***Rimbey***, James N. (1996):

THE ECONOMIC CONSEQUENCES OF ACCOUNTING FOR STOCK SPLITS AND LARGE STOCK DIVIDENDS, in: "The Accounting Review", Vol. 71, 1996, Issue 2, 241-253.

Powell, Gary E.; ***Baker***, H. Kent (1993):

THE EFFECTS OF STOCK SPLITS ON THE OWNERSHIP MIX OF A FIRM, in: "Review of Financial Economics", Vol. 3, 1993, 70-88.

Rankine, Graeme W.; ***Stice***, Eearl K. (1997a):

ACCOUNTING RULES AND THE SIGNALING PROPERTIES OF 20 PERCENT STOCK DIVIDENDS, in: "Accounting Review", Vol. 72, 1997, Issue 1, 23-46.

Rankine, Graeme; ***Stice***, Eearl K. (1997b):

THE MARKET REACTION TO THE CHOICE OF ACCOUNTING METHOD FOR STOCK SPLITS AND LARGE STOCK DIVIDENDS, in: "Journal of Financial & Quantitative Analysis", Vol. 32, 1997, Issue 2, 161-182.

Roberts, Michael L.; ***Samson***, William D.; ***Dugan***, Michael T. (1990):

THE STOCKHOLDERS' EQUITY SECTION: FORM WITHOUT SUBSTANCE?, in: "Accounting Horizons", Vol. 4, 1990, Issue 4, 35-46.

Röder, Klaus (1999):

KURSWIRKUNGEN VON MELDUNGEN DEUTSCHER AKTIENGESELLSCHAFTEN, in: "Reihe: Quantitative Ökonomie", Vol. 98, 1999, Josef Eul Verlag, Cologne.

Ross, Stephen A. (1977):

THE DETERMINATION OF FINANCIAL STRUCTURE: THE INCENTIVE-SIGNALLING APPROACH, in: "Bell Journal of Economics", Vol. 8, 1977, Issue 1, 23-40.

Schulz, Harald (1972):

DER EINFLUSS VON KAPITALERHÖHUNGEN AUS GESELLSCHAFTSMITTELN AUF DIE ENTWICKLUNG DER AKTIENKURSE, Verlag Otto Schwartz & Co, 1972, Göttingen.

Sharpe, William F. (1963):

A SIMPLIFIED MODEL FOR PORTFOLIO ANALYSIS, in: "Management Science", Vol. 9, 1963, Issue 2, 277-293.

Sharpe, William F. (1964):

CAPITAL ASSET PRICES: A THEORY OF MARKET EQUILIBRIUM UNDER CONDITIONS OF RISK, in: "Journal of Finance", Vol. 19, Issue 3, 425-442.

Smith, Clifford W., ***Warner***, Jerold B. (1979):

ON FINANCIAL CONTRACTING: AN ANALYSIS OF BOND COVENANTS, in: "Journal of Financial Economics", Vol. 7, 1979, Issue 2, 117-161.

Spence, Michael (1973):

JOB MARKET SIGNALING, in: "Quarterly Journal of Economics", Vol. 87, 1973, Issue 3, 355-374.

Strong, Norman (1992):

MODELLING ABNORMAL RETURNS: A REVIEW ARTICLE, in: "Journal of Business Finance & Accounting", Vol. 19, 1992, Issue 4, 533-553.

Wilcoxon, Frank (1945):

INDIVIDUAL COMPARISONS BY RANKING METHODS, in: "Biometrics Bulletin", Vol. 1, 1945, Issue 6, 80-83.

Woolridge, J. Randall (1983a):

EX-DATE STOCK PRICE ADJUSTMENT TO STOCK DIVIDENDS, in: "Journal of Finance", Vol. 38, 1983, Issue 1, 247-255.

Woolridge, J. Randall (1983b):

STOCK DIVIDENDS AS SIGNALS, in: "Journal of Financial Research", Vol. 6, 1983, Issue 1, 1-12.

Woolridge, J. Randall; ***Chambers***, Donald R. (1983):

REVERSE SPLITS AND SHAREHOLDER WEALTH, in: "Financial Management (1972)", Vol. 12, 1983, Issue 3, 5-15.

Wulff, Christian (2001):

KAPITALMARKTREAKTIONEN AUF NENNWERTUMSTELLUNGEN, in: "Empirische Finanzmarktforschung", Gabler Edition Wissenschaft, 2001, Wiesbaden.

Wulff, Christian (2002):

THE MARKET REACTION TO STOCK SPLITS – EVIDENCE FROM GERMANY, in: "Schmalenbach Business Review", Vol. 54, 2002, Issue 3, 270-297.

Studienreihe der Stiftung Kreditwirtschaft an der Universität Hohenheim

Bände 1 - 11 sind nicht mehr lieferbar.

Band 12: Axel Tibor Kümmel: Bewertung von Kreditinstituten nach dem Shareholder Value Ansatz, 1994; 2. Aufl.; 1995.

Band 13: Petra Schmidt: Insider Trading. Maßnahmen zur Vermeidung bei US-Banken; 1995.

Band 14: Alexander Grupp: Börseneintritt und Börsenaustritt. Individuelle und institutionelle Interessen; 1995.

Band 15: Heinrich Kerstien: Budgetierung in Kreditinstituten. Operative Ergebnisplanung auf der Basis entscheidungsorientierter Kalkulationsverfahren; 1995.

Band 16: Ulrich Gärtner: Die Kalkulation des Zinspositionserfolgs in Kreditinstituten; 1996.

Band 17: Ute Münstermann: Märkte für Risikokapital im Spannungsfeld von Organisationsfreiheit und Staatsaufsicht; 1996.

Band 18: Ulrike Müller: Going Public im Geschäftsfeld der Banken. Marktbetrachtungen, bankbezogene Anforderungen und Erfolgswirkungen; 1997.

Band 19: Daniel Reith: Innergenossenschaftlicher Wettbewerb im Bankensektor; 1997.

Band 20: Steffen Hörter: Shareholder Value-orientiertes Bank-Controlling; 1998.

Band 21: Philip von Boehm-Bezing: Eigenkapital für nicht börsennotierte Unternehmen durch Finanzintermediäre. Wirtschaftliche Bedeutung und institutionelle Rahmenbedingungen; 1998.

Band 22: Niko J. Kleinmann: Die Ausgestaltung der Ad-hoc-Publizität nach § 15 WpHG. Notwendigkeit einer segmentspezifischen Deregulierung; 1998.

Band 23: Elke Ebert: Startfinanzierung durch Kreditinstitute. Situationsanalyse und Lösungsansätze; 1998.

Band 24: Heinz O. Steinhübel: Die private Computerbörse für mittelständische Unternehmen. Ökonomische Notwendigkeit und rechtliche Zulässigkeit; 1998.

Band 25: Reiner Dietrich: Integrierte Kreditprüfung. Die Integration der computergestützten Kreditprüfung in die Gesamtbanksteuerung; 1998.

Band 26: Stefan Topp: Die Pre-Fusionsphase von Kreditinstituten. Eine Untersuchung der Entscheidungsprozesse und ihrer Strukturen; 1999.

Band 27: Bettina Korn: Vorstandsvergütung mit Aktienoptionen. Sicherung der Anreizkompatibilität als gesellschaftsrechtliche Gestaltungsaufgabe; 2000.

Band 28: Armin Lindtner: Asset Backed Securities – Ein Cash flow-Modell; 2001.

Band 29: Carsten Lausberg: Das Immobilienmarktrisiko deutscher Banken; 2001.

Band 30: Patrik Pohl: Risikobasierte Kapitalanforderungen als Instrument einer marktorientierten Bankenaufsicht – unter besonderer Berücksichtigung der bankaufsichtlichen Behandlung des Kreditrisikos; 2001.

Band 31: Joh. Heinr. von Stein/Friedrich Trautwein: Ausbildungscontrolling an Universitäten. Grundlagen, Implementierung und Perspektiven; 2002.

Band 32: Gaby Kienzler, Christiane Winz: Ausbildungsqualität bei Bankkaufleuten – aus der Sicht von Auszubildenden und Ausbildern, 2002.

Band 33: Joh. Heinr. von Stein, Holger G. Köckritz, Friedrich Trautwein (Hrsg.): E-Banking im Privatkundengeschäft. Eine Analyse strategischer Handlungsfelder, 2002.

Band 34: Antje Erndt, Steffen Metzner: Moderne Instrumente des Immobiliencontrollings. DCF-Bewertung und Kennzahlensysteme im Immobiliencontrolling, 2002.

Band 35: Sven A. Röckle: Schadensdatenbanken als Instrument zur Quantifizierung von Operational Risk in Kreditinstituten, 2002.

Band 36: Frank Kutschera: Kommunales Debt Management als Bankdienstleistung, 2003.

Band 37: Niklas Lach: Marktinformation durch Bankrechnungslegung im Dienste der Bankenaufsicht, 2003.

Band 38: Wigbert Böhm: Investor Relations der Emittenten von Unternehmensanleihen: Notwendigkeit, Nutzen und Konzeption einer gläubigerorientierten Informationspolitik, 2004.

Band 39: Andreas Russ: Kapitalmarktorientiertes Kreditrisikomanagement in der prozessbezogenen Kreditorganisation, 2004.

Band 40: Tim Arndt: Manager of Managers – Verträge. Outsourcing im Rahmen individueller Finanzportfolioverwaltung von Kredit- und Finanzdienstleistungsinstituten, 2004

Band 41: Manuela A. E. Schäfer: Prozessgetriebene multiperspektivische Unternehmenssteuerung: Beispielhafte Betrachtung anhand der deutschen Bausparkassen, 2004.

Band 42: Friedrich Trautwein: Berufliche Handlungskompetenz als Studienziel: Bedeutung, Einflussfaktoren und Förderungsmöglichkeiten beim betriebswirtschaftlichen Studium an Universitäten unter besonderer Berücksichtigung der Bankwirtschaft, 2004.

Band 43: Ekkehardt Anton Bauer: Theorie der staatlichen Venture Capital-Politik. Begründungsansätze, Wirkungen und Effizienz der staatlichen Subventionierung von Venture Capital, 2006.

Band 44: Ralf Kürten: Regionale Finanzplätze in Deutschland, 2006.

Band 45: Tatiana Glaser: Privatimmobilienfinanzierung in Russland und Möglichkeiten der Übertragung des deutschen Bausparsystems auf die Russische Föderation anhand des Beispiels von Sankt Petersburg, 2006.

Band 46: Elisabeth Doris Markel: Qualitative Bankenaufsicht. Auswirkungen auf die Bankunternehmungsführung, 2010.

Band 47: Matthias Johannsen: Stock Price Reaction to Earnings Information, 2010.

Band 48: Susanna Holzschneider: Valuationa and Underpricing of Initial Public Offerings, 2011.

Band 49: Arne Breuer: An Empirical Analysis of Order Dynamics in a High-Frequency Trading Environment, 2013.

Band 50: Dirk Sturz: Stock Dividends in Germany. An Empirical Analysis, 2015.